W9-BLZ-973

Submarines, Technology, and History

Selected Articles by
John Merrill

Copyright © 2004 by John Merrill

All rights reserved. No part of this book shall be reproduced or transmitted in any form or by any means, electronic, mechanical, magnetic, photographic including photocopying, recording or by any information storage and retrieval system, without prior written permission of the publisher. No patent liability is assumed with respect to the use of the information contained herein. Although every precaution has been taken in the preparation of this book, the publisher and author assume no responsibility for errors or omissions. Neither is any liability assumed for damages resulting from the use of the information contained herein.

ISBN 0-7414-1812-6

Published by:

INFI∞ITY
PUBLISHING.COM

519 West Lancaster Avenue
Haverford, PA 19041-1413
Info@buybooksontheweb.com
www.buybooksontheweb.com
Toll-free (877) BUY BOOK
Local Phone (610) 520-2500
Fax (610) 519-0261

Printed in the United States of America

Printed on Recycled Paper

Published March 2004

Submarines, Technology, and History

Following the author's career in Navy research and development related to submarine systems, these historical monographs represent a post-career interest in exploring the history and telling the story of the development and implementation of several submarine or submarine-related technologies. Historical research led to investigation of convoying merchant ships during both World Wars. An interest in sonobuoys brought P.M.S. Blackett and his broad contributions to science, antisubmarine warfare and operations research to the author's attention.

Several of the papers present the only public record of the creativity of some individual engineers and scientists and their contributions to the United States Navy. In most of the papers submarines provide a common thread. With some exceptions, events of the 20th Century predominate.

Part I articles are presented in the order in which they appeared in *The Submarine Review* starting in 1993. The *Review* is the quarterly publication of the Naval Submarine League, a professional organization for submariners and submarine advocates founded in 1982. The quarterly journal provides a forum for exchange of thoughts on submarine matters. The monographs are reprinted with permission from the Naval Submarine League.

Part II consists of two articles that appeared in *Naval History*. This periodical, sponsored by the U.S. Naval Institute, is in its seventeenth year and presents articles about historical discoveries, first-person accounts, and interviews by notable naval veterans and historians. The articles from *Naval History* are reprinted with permission from the Naval Institute.

Part III includes articles on the World War II research efforts at the Harvard Underwater Sound Laboratory and the University of California Laboratory at Point Loma, California. They appeared in the spring 1994 issue of the IEEE Oceanic Engineering Society Newsletter.

CONTENTS

Part I
The Submarine Review

Part II
Naval History

Sonobuoy	Jan,/Feb. 1994	111
From the Heavens to the Depths: Astronomer George E. Hale Attacks U-boats with Technology	June 2000	119

Part III
Other Publications

Harvard Underwater Sound Laboratory	IEEE Oceanic Engineering Society Newsletter	Spring 1994	130
University of California Division of War Research at San Diego	IEEE Oceanic Engineering Society Newsletter	Spring 1994	135

To Captain James C. Hay (USN retired):

You provided the opportunity and the articles happened.

John Merrill

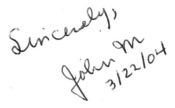

Sincerely,
John M
3/22/04

Part I

The Submarine Review

Fort Trumbull-A Navy High Technology Site

Colonial Period

In 1775, with increased military action against the colonies by the British, the Connecticut Council of Safety recommended fortifications be built for the town of New London on the west bank of the Thames River and Groton on the east bank. At that time, New London with a population of about five thousand was the third largest town in the Connecticut Colony.

During the next two years, two earthworks type forts were constructed by relays of citizens and recruits from the countryside. The fort on the New London side was located about two miles north of the mouth of the river where it flows into Long Island Sound. The fort site on the east side of the river on Groton Heights was opposite and just slightly to the north. This first New London fort was south of the town. Today, the fort area is surrounded by New London on both the south and west. The rocky point location for the fort rises at some places to about thirty-five feet above the riverbank. In early times, the location was called Point Mamacock. Later it was some times referred to as Fort Neck.

It has been suggested that in 1637 the same site was the location of the first English houses in the area which later became New London. The house or houses are said to have been built at the initiative of a Captain Stoughton. In June 1637, Stoughton with one hundred twenty men from Massachusetts Bay Colony arrived at Pequot Harbor (New London) on an expedition to exterminate if possible the Pequot Indians.

The fort on the New London side of the river was a rectangle about eighty feet on a side with earthworks on the north, east and south sides and open to the west. The heavy cannon were cast in Salisbury, Connecticut, about 75 miles away in the northwest corner of the colony near the New York line. The first fort at Point Mamacock was named in December 1776 for the current governor of Connecticut, Jonathan Trumbull. The fort on the high ground on the east bank in Groton was named Fort Griswold for the then deputy governor, Matthew Griswold.

Fort Trumbull was manned and in March 1778 was strengthened and repaired, while additional batteries were added. On September 6, 1781, Benedict Arnold, British brigadier general, led an expedition against Forts Trumbull and Griswold. Arnold, a native of nearby Norwich, Connecticut, and former Continental Army brigadier general, was well acquainted with the locale. Captain Adam Shapley, Fort Trumbull's Captain of Artillery, shot one volley, then followed orders to spike his guns. He then took his 23 men across the river to aid Fort Griswold, which was also under siege. Less than a month later on October 19, the British armies surrendered at Yorktown, Virginia.

After the Revolution, Fort Trumbull continued under the aegis of Connecticut. During President Washington's second term, in 1794, Sieur de Rochefontaine, who fought with Washington's Continental Army, was appointed civilian engineer to fortify certain harbors along the coast including

2

New London, Connecticut. Money was authorized by the 3rd Congress to upgrade the Fort. Details of garrisoning for both peace and war were established. In October 1798, the Connecticut General Assembly ceded the Fort to the United States Army. This stewardship continued until 1910.

Nineteenth Century

Starting in the 1830s, the United States undertook the building of a series of strategically located forts. The forts were to provide long-term security against invasion. Collectively they were referred to as the *permanent system.*

A new Fort Trumbull was included in this new fort system. It was to be located in the area nearby the site of the 1775/77 Revolutionary fort. It was located on a hillock slightly south of the original construction. The new fort would be constructed of granite from the nearby quarries and in the Egyptian Revival style which was popular at the time. Increased land was purchased for the War Department by an Act of Congress. Further land was also ceded to the United States. By the end of the century, the total area of the fort was about twenty acres.

Senate appropriations in the order of $400,000 were approved in 1836 for the new fort. Construction of the granite fort was begun in 1836 and completed in 1854. An original painting of the fort by Seth Eastman in the 1870-75 period was hung in the Capitol in Washington, DC.

As the century moved on, Fort Trumbull was overtaken by technological events. Coast artillery to resist invasion changed in capabilities such as range and placement. New forts and emplacements moved closer to the sea. After the turn of century, Fort Trumbull and adjoining real estate became available government property.

Twentieth Century

Fort Trumbull and the adjacent acreage have coves on the north and south sides of the promontory. The coves are manageable for small boats, and piers on the river can accommodate a wide range of ships. Extensive nautical use of the fort area began in 1910 with the arrival of the United States Revenue Cutter Service at Fort Trumbull.

Revenue Cutter Service ships, shore personnel and cadet corps became the primary tenant at Fort Trumbull. The following year, this use of the Fort Trumbull area was formalized with a transfer of Fort Trumbull from the War Department to the Treasury Department. In 1914, the Revenue Cutter Service's officer school at the fort was designated as the service's academy. This location for the academy was used until 1932, when the present United States Coast Guard Academy was opened at a site also on the west bank of the Thames River in New London, about two miles further north. Overall, the Coast Guard has had a continuous presence since 1910. The kind, size and scale of the activities have varied.

World War I

After the outbreak of World War I in August 1914, Germany's first merchant steamship sinking by submarine occurred October 26, 1914, bringing attention to this form of warfare. America's attitude toward the German U-boat sinkings hardened when on May 17, 1915, the British liner *Lusitania,* on its way from New York to Liverpool, was sunk off the coast of Ireland by two torpedoes fired from the German submarine U-20. The Lusitania sank in twenty minutes. In the sinking, over one thousand lives were lost including 128 United States citizens.

Concern regarding the U-boat menace and United States military preparedness led to establishing of the Naval

Consulting Board in July, 1915. The Board brought together some of country's senior inventors and engineers (including Thomas Edison) to address technology problems including antisubmarine considerations. The Board's structure and deliberations did not include the membership of either the American Physical Society (physicists) or the National Academy of Sciences.

The U-boat sinkings continued, and by the end of 1916 Germany had 102 U-boats. During 1915 and 1916, unrestricted German submarine warfare by the U-boats was an off-on affair somewhat dependent upon the American diplomatic pressures and their reception by the German government and military.

The Naval Consulting Board addressed the submarine threat with a Special Problems Committee investigating submarine detection. By 1917, a research activity for the development of sound detection devices was in operation on the coast of Massachusetts east of Boston at Nahant. Industrial scientists and engineers from General Electric, American Telephone & Telegraph and the Boston-based Submarine Signal Company were engaged in the research and development efforts.

New London Area 1917

The declaration of war against Germany on April 6, 1917, generally increased the scope and scale of several activities in the area. The Navy with twenty first-line submarines instituted the United States Navy Submarine School in Groton across the river from New London at the site of the Navy's New London Coaling Station. The Coast Guard transfer to the Navy for the duration of the war increased the activity at Fort Trumbull. The Electric Boat

Company[1], a submarine builder since the turn of the century, owned a subsidiary in Groton, the New London Ship and Engine Company. Diesel engines for ships and submarines had been produced at that location since 1911. Orders for submarine diesel engines for new construction for both United States and Great Britain provided further stimulus to the industrial activity in the region.

National Academy of Sciences (NAS)

A year earlier, George Ellery Hale, one of the country's leading academic scientists as spokesman for the National Academy of Sciences, offered the services of the membership to President Wilson. Until this time, the academic physicists had not been involved in the search for solutions to military technological problems. In April 1916, the President accepted the Academy's offer to help. In response the NAS set up the National Research Council made up of some NAS members and military representatives.

On January 9, 1917, Germany renewed its unrestricted submarine campaign. The following month the Navy asked the National Research Council to develop submarine detection devices. The committee addressing this effort was chaired by Robert A. Millikan, a well known physicist from the University of Chicago on duty as an Army officer. By the end of June 1917, the Navy authorized the National Research Council to start research at New London with a staff of academic professors. An initial staff of six academic scientists and Millikan met at the Mohican Hotel in New London to discuss a submarine detection device that had been recently brought from France. The academic scientists who came to the Fort Trumbull area to work

---

[1] Construction of submarines at the Groton location by the Electric Boat Company began in 1925.

occupied buildings on the cove south of the Coast Guard facilities at Fort Trumbull.

Fiscal support for the initial research and salaries at New London was from academic and professional scientific organizations. Vannevar Bush, one of the researchers, was supported for his work in New London on submarine detection equipment by the J. P. Morgan firm. Academic institutions represented included Harvard, McGill, Yale, Wesleyan, MIT, Cornell, Chicago, Rice, Columbia, and Swarthmore.

By early July 1917, Max Mason, a member of the New London research team and a mathematician from the University of Wisconsin, had conducted experiments both in the lake at Madison, Wisconsin, and on a dock at New London with an underwater sound detector he invented. This detector was considered in some circles at the end of the hostilities to be the best of those available to the allied navies. Many of the researchers had come to New London from significant scientific and academic careers and after the closing of the research activity in late 1918 went on to continuing scientific achievement in several fields of science. Two would receive Nobel prizes, R. A. Millikan in 1923 and P. W. Bridgman in 1926.

President Roosevelt, as Assistant Secretary of the Navy during World War I, also had involvement with the research activities at Fort Trumbull. Early government support for the work was limited. In October 1917, Roosevelt was concerned with the transfer of funds for research on submarine detection devices. The Navy released $300,000 in support of the research. On October 12, the Navy took over the research effort; and the location was designated the Navy Experimental Station at New London.

Research and experiments at the Station included Navy aircraft and dirigibles. The seaplanes were located at the cove south of the Fort. Training Navy personnel to operate the shipboard detection equipment, listeners school, was another aspect of the activities at Fort Trumbull. By November 1918, the Station included laboratories and test facilities for thirty-two professors, three submarine chasers, three yachts, a destroyer and more than 700 enlisted men.

A destroyer, *USS Jouett (DD-41)*, arrived at New London on January 15, 1918, for experimentation with antisubmarine devices. The *Jouett* was fitted with the most sophisticated World War I non-electric binaural listening system. The destroyer was able to track a target submarine at ranges of 500 to 2,000 yards while it was operating at speeds of 20 knots.

In 1950, in his autobiography, Millikan observed regarding the Experimental Station, "long before the war closed the New London Station had practically absorbed the Nahant Station and become one great center of antisubmarine and other naval experimenting, all done after the beginning of 1918."

The Fort Trumbull site for the submarine detection research provided a waterside location with reasonable access to open water and proximity to the Navy's Submarine School across the river several miles to the north, while the Electric Boat Company's submarine engine subsidiary was within view on the east bank of the river in Groton.

The end of the war in November was followed by the closing of the Navy Experimental Station. However, many of the assemblage of scientists who comprised the resident, visiting and technical managers of the research at Fort Trumbull would during the next two decades grow in stature and prominence at both the national and international levels, some in academia and some in industry. In 1940, when the submarine threat again became more menacing, they provided the core of the leadership which returned the Fort Trumbull area to a high technology site.

A theme promulgated by Hale in engaging scientists' participation in the war effort was the need for independence in the work in support of the military. A. Hunter Dupree, in his 1957 Science in the Federal Government, noted "As the war went on, more and more of the NRC's program went over to military control...less capable of initiating projects, depending increasingly on the assumption that the military knew what to ask for." The need for independence was not lost on Vannevar Bush, one of the 1917-18 researchers, in 1940 as he organized the national scientific and engineering resources to meet the German threat.

Fort Trumbull Experimental Station
Antisubmarine Warfare Planes 1917-18

Courtesy of David Shippee

S-20 First submarine detected from the air using a sonobuoy

March 1942

P.M.S. BLACKETT
NAVAL OFFICER, NOBEL PRIZE WINNER, SUBMARINE HUNTER

Patrick Maynard Stuart Blackett, born 18 November 1897 in Kensington, London, was the son of a stockbroker. At thirteen, he entered Osborne Royal Naval College and in 1912 transferred to the Dartmouth Royal Naval College. Throughout World War I, he served at sea, initially as a naval cadet, and saw action in the battle of the Falkland Islands in 1914 and the battle of Jutland in 1916. Promoted to the rank of lieutenant in May 1918, the Admiralty sent him to study at Cambridge in January of 1919. He liked the Cavendish Laboratory and resigned from the Navy to continue his studies there as a civilian. After passing the final honors examination in mathematics in May 1919, he passed the physics final honors examination two years later.

Among his teachers at Cambridge was Lord Ernest Rutherford, one of England's greatest physicists. Rutherford won the Nobel Prize in 1909, and in 1919 had just been appointed Cavendish Professor of Experimental Physics at the university. As a student and after completing his physics studies in 1921, Blackett participated in experiments under Rutherford exploring the possibility of the artificial transmutation of the elements by alpha particle bombardment. For 10 years, he continued at the Cavendish Laboratory with Rutherford, who suggested that Blackett consider working on an improved version of the Wilson cloud chamber.

Blackett's Nobel laureate in 1948 was for the further development of the cloud chamber and discoveries in the field of nuclear physics and cosmic radiation. Earlier in 1946, he was awarded the highest award the United States can make to a civilian, the Medal for Merit. This was for his operational work in connection with the anti-U-boat campaign during the war.

His varied roles as a civilian in the technological aspects of warfare started in the mid-1930s. Along with his highly regarded scientific acumen, Blackett brought a deep understanding of the system aspects of successful weaponry and the application of scientific analysis to the operations of war.

Blackett firmly grasped the importance of the relationships and understandings between the scientist and the equipment end user, the military. He understood the significance of collecting reliable data on the results of weapon usage as the essence of determining equipment performance. This was another aspect of Blackett's effective application of scientific methods and the use of statistics to wartime technological problem solving.

During mid-January 1935, Blackett was appointed to serve on the Committee for the Scientific Survey of Air Defense, under the chairmanship of Sir Henry Tizard, who had been selected to head the Committee the previous year. The Committee's purpose was "to consider how far recent advances in scientific and technical knowledge can be used to strengthen the present methods of defence against hostile aircraft." [1] During its five-year existence, the support and implementation of radar stands out as one of the Committee's important contributions. When war came in 1939, the whole east and southeast coast of England had

---

[1] P.M.S. Blackett, Studies of War---Nuclear and Conventional, Hill and Wang, New York, 1952, p. 102.

operational radar chains. This was one of the factors in winning the Battle of Britain in 1940.

In the beginning of World War II Blackett joined the instrument section of the Royal Aircraft Establishment at Fainborough, where he made a major contribution to the Mk 14 bombsight for the Royal air Force. This bombsight, brought to completion by another scientist, removed the need for a level run before bomb release and was in use by the Bomber Command from 1942 until the end of the war.

By August 1940, Blackett was the science advisor at the headquarters of the Anti-Aircraft Command at Stanmore. Here he was involved in studies and analysis to enhance the use of radar to direct gunfire. The analysis team for gun-laying radars included a physiologist, an astronomer, a mathematician and physicists. The results led to a significant reduction from 20,000 to 4,000 in the number of rounds needed to down an enemy plane.

The magnitude of the U-boat problem and need to address a range of solutions directed his assignment in March of 1941 to the Operational Research Section of Coastal Command. His duties included studies of methods of attack and determination of the proper depth for depth charge explosions on submarines. Studies regarding planned flying and maintenance of Coastal Command aircraft resulted in a doubling of the flying hours per month for a given number of planes and personnel. To Blackett and his operational research colleagues is attributed the concept of painting the submarine-searching planes white instead of a dark color to lessen the opportunity for a U-boat to discern patrolling planes against the background of the sky.

In May 1941, Blackett wrote a memorandum proposing a detector buoy astern of convoys to detect shadowing or trailing enemy submarines acoustically and then to transmit the information by radio to the ship.[2] At about the same time, J. T. Tate and L. B. Slichter of the United States National Defense Research Committee heard of the idea while in Great Britain on an exchange mission concerning anti-submarine devices. This ultimately led the following year to the development of the sonobuoy at Columbia University's Underwater Sound Laboratory in New London. The sonobuoy met with success during the war and to the present continues to play an important role in current anti-submarine warfare.

Additionally, Blackett's wartime interests included analysis of the strategic value of aircraft, escort duty on convoys, general sweeps over the Atlantic, patrolling of the Bay of Biscay, and effectiveness of 10-cm radar. By June 1943, the U-boat menace was somewhat mastered.

After the war, Blackett's career continued at the University of Manchester where he had become Professor of Physics in 1937. He established a school of cosmic ray research and stimulated the development of other research interests, which led to the creation of the first chair of radio astronomy at the University of Manchester and to the building of the Jodrell Bank Experimental Station for radio astronomy 20 miles south of Manchester. Construction started in 1952 and the station was in operation by the fall of 1957. It has one of the world's largest fully steerable radio telescopes with a reflector 250 feet in diameter.

Blackett's scientific and technical interests were broad, ranging from work with magnetometers and measurement of the magnetic properties of rocks back 500 million years in time, to conceptual thinking about the continental drift theory. In 1945, he worked at the highest

---

[2] W. Hackman, Seek & Strike: Sonar, Anti-Submarine Warfare and the Royal Navy 1914-45, London, Her Majesty's Stationery Office, 1984, p. 395.

government levels to support the development of a computer industry. He became president of the Royal Society in 1965, an appropriate acknowledgment of his many talents.

A final note: Blackett is reported to have been kicking off at a student's football match when he was informed of his winning the Nobel Prize.

Submarine Radio Communications 1900-1945

[Author's Acknowledgement: This paper is heavily dependent on many sources. However, special note is made of Evolution of Naval Radio-Electronics and Contributions of the Naval Research Laboratory *by Louis A. Gebhard. This book helped to clarify many technical developments at NRL that improved submarine radio communications.]*

In the winter of 1896-97, John P. Holland's sixth submarine, which would become *USS Holland (SS 1)* on April 11, 1900, began to take shape at Nixon's Crescent Shipyard, Elizabeth, New Jersey.

At the same time 24-year-old Guglielmo Marconi, recently from Italy, was in England demonstrating his wireless equipment and taking out his first patent. Returning to Italy in June 1897, Marconi established wireless communications from land to Italian warships located at distances of up to some 10 miles. By 1902, on the United States liner *Philadelphia* en route to the United States, he was receiving wireless messages at distances of 700 miles during the day and 1500 miles at night. Customers for his system of wireless telegraphy included various navies and armies as well as the commercial sector. These achievements in wireless telegraphy led to his Nobel Prize for Physics in 1909.

Naval Communications in 1896

Communications between ships at sea was considered a knotty problem in 1896 when Marconi was demonstrating his early wireless communications in England. Later in 1922, a retired United States Navy captain relating the history and development of radio or wireless telegraphy looked back to his time at the Naval War College in 1896 and summarized ship communication then.

"Outside the use of carrier pigeons, the sense of sight and hearing only were under consideration, that is, visual or audible communications between ships in extended formation...searchlight reflection on clouds at night...30 mile communication sent and answered. A signal gun was estimated to be audible at 10 miles if conditions were favorable."

The captain went on to note that by 1901-02 (after the Spanish War), Marconi's concept of wireless communication between naval vessels up to 50 miles apart was achieved.

On 21 January 1900, the *New York Herald* reported "the day of flag and lamp signaling system in the Navy is drawing to a close." At this time, Navy Board considerations included the advisability of discontinuing the homing pigeon service and evaluating wireless radio. The Navy Board reported favorably for the wireless. The next year, 1901, the Bureau of Equipment bought duplicate wireless sets from France, Germany, Britain, and from the DeForest Company in the United States. Two years later 45 more sets were procured.

With wireless transmitting ranges of the order of 74 miles, the Royal Navy by 1900 had 26 ships equipped with wireless and six coast stations constructed. The British were the first to equip submarines with wireless telegraphy. The

British submarine *Holland 1*, laid down in February 1901 with sea trials in April 1902, had a wireless compartment.

Military application in wartime quickly followed. During one of the final sea engagements between Russia and Japan in the northern Pacific on May 27, 1905, in a lifting fog at 3:30 AM the captain of the armed merchant cruiser *Shinano Maru* used wireless radio to his advantage. He sighted the Russian fleet and, using the wireless, within 90 minutes was able to bring four of Japan's finest battleships on a course to intercept the Russians and successfully destroy the opposing fleet. Without relay, the Japanese were generally able to communicate to ranges of about 60 miles.

General use of radio by the United States Navy in 1906 finds 57 equipped ships, 39 shore stations, and a transmit-receive capability between surface ships of about 640 miles. The primary wireless use at this time was for fleet reporting and ship-to-shore and vice versa, with additional support on land by use of the telegraph. Visual communication methods were still somewhat preferred. During this period, good operating discipline among naval wireless operators was generally lacking; this did not contribute to a broad acceptance of wireless.

Radio communication with submarines remained operationally unsatisfactory for several more decades. Space available in the submarine for radio equipment was limited, the power capability of the available transmitters was low, and the small antennas were too short for the low radio frequencies and equipment available through the 1920s.

An Early 1907 View of the Submarine and Wireless Telegraphy

In 1907, Cyprian Bridge, an officer in the Royal Navy (later Admiral Sir Cyprian Bridge), wrote "Why do we want submarine boats? To do with increasing of invisibility, but otherwise under greater difficulties the same work as torpedo-boats, viz., to sink or injure an enemy's ships." Regarding radio-telegraphy, Bridge observed, "It permits between an observer and his chief, scores and perhaps hundreds of miles apart, the exchange of question and answer…the range of direct communication has already been increased to twenty times its former amount, if not still more."

To assure better wireless equipment performance from the manufacturers, the Navy established the U. S. Naval RadioTelegraph Laboratories in the fall of 1908 under the Navy's Bureau of Equipment. Working space and facilities were made available at the National Bureau of Standards in Washington, DC. Further performance needs led the Navy by 1915 to develop radio equipment in house. The Washington Navy Yard was assigned the development of radio receivers and wave meters. Naval Laboratories at various locations such as Great Lakes, Illinois and the Naval Air Station at Washington (Anacostia), DC addressed research and development aspects of the Navy's radio needs during and immediately after World War I. The efforts included radio broadcasting, radio detection and aircraft radio.

At the time Bridge was making his observations, both the United States and Great Britain had already accepted the notion of the submarine primarily for coastal defense. In 1908, British D-boats appeared with radio masts, the first for a British submarine. Cage type antennas were slung from the masts.

By 1910, the number of German submarines began noticeably to increase. Starting with the outfitting of the U-5 in June 1910, all further U-boats were fitted with radiotelegraphy. On the U-5, two aerial masts could be lowered from inside the submarine. The wireless system communication distances achieved were about 50-62 nautical miles between ships and U-boats and distances of about 30 nautical miles between U-boats. British submarine radio distance performance matched that of the U-boats.

With the beginning of World War I hostilities, 45 U-boats were ready for service or in construction. The Royal Navy submarine fleet was the largest in the world with 74 boats, 31 under construction and 14 more either on order or projected.

In the last pre-war British maneuvers of 1913, the submarine was perceived by some as having greater possibilities than those of harbor defense. Two distinct roles for the submarine began to evolve: those of submarine killer and of a fast long-range cruiser-like underwater support of the line of battle.

Communications with and among military ships at sea through the centuries has always been a continuing unwieldy problem. Even with all the current technological advances at the start of the 20th century, surface ship wireless communications were only embryonic in view of the progress in wireless communications which the new century would bring. Although the 1901 annual report of Secretary of the Navy John D. Long referred to the advisability of discontinuing the homing pigeon service and substituting for it some system of wireless, World War I would still see the use of this mode to pass information from a submarine to the shore base.

An often-encountered story tells of a British E class submarine operating off Heligoland, the German North Sea Gibraltar-like naval base. The need arose for the submarine to send an urgent message to Harwich, a homeport for destroyer and submarine flotillas on the east coast of England 140 miles from the submarine. The submarine's wireless telegraph range was 50 miles. The submarine captain at 4 AM ordered four pigeons, each carrying identical words, to be dispatched in a moderate wind for Harwich in a west-south-westerly direction. The message arrived at about 3:30 in the afternoon. This took place almost 20 years after Marconi's development. Communications were certainly among the submariner's problems.

The need for enhanced submarine communications would soon be apparent, but the technologies to achieve this would only slowly evolve. The surface ship's communication dilemma by the mid-1920s would be under reasonable control. The solution to submarine wireless communication problems through and beyond World War I would lag. Reasons for the lag stemmed in part from the immediate environment and proximity of the sea to the submarine and its appurtenances.

Through the years, submarine antenna problems due to temperature (from the tropics to the Arctic regions), pressure as the submarine went deeper, drag forces as it moved faster, wave slap, and high sea states always ranked high. Adding to these primarily mechanical challenges, the sea around the submarine is generally opaque to the radio waves. Notwithstanding these realities, the submarine gradually became electromagnetically connected although sometimes the pace was imperceptible. In retrospect, the slowness was due to a combination of shortfalls in understanding, technological developments, and fiscal allocations.

At the beginning of World War I in 1914, one would find both wireless and diesel engine for propulsion as innovations in the E class, the fifth evolution of U. S. Navy submarines.

A 1915 book regarding modern submarines and their role in naval warfare at that time prompted the comment that radio (day or night) means of signaling was first in a list of eight techniques or methods of signaling. That same year, author Frederick A. Talbot observed that German boats were using wireless telegraph to relay 150 miles to Berlin. In 1916, the U-20 (which had sunk the *Lusitania* the previous year) established a submarine distance wireless record of 770 miles, communicating with Germany. In March of the following year after sinking a French battleship off Sardinia in the Mediterranean, the U-64 reported that event that same night to a German cruiser operating off the coast of northwest Germany. This was accomplished with a transmitter power of about 1 kilowatt and telescopic aerial masts. U-boats operating against commerce west of the British Isles routinely were able to talk directly with stations in Germany and Belgium.

The concept of a fleet submarine in support of the battle group grew. This was articulated in 1916 by Lieutenant (junior grade) F. A. Daubin in *The Fleet Submarine*, an article in the <u>Naval Institute Proceedings</u>. Daubin observed that by February 1916, 487 ships had been sunk by submarines. He discussed the characteristics of a fleet submarine and noted that the increased size of the fleet boat would allow for a radio plant of greater power than the limited space available in the then current coast defense submarines. This fleet concept persisted for next several decades and heavily influenced submarine design. The evolving role of an independent offensive submarine brought the submarine further into the command and control communications needs. From 1915, anti-submarine warfare was the primary submarine mission.

A 1917 book, <u>Secrets of the Submarine</u>, mentioned that the submarine wireless problem was one of antenna masts. At that time experiments with telescopic and folding masts, mounting and dismounting without crew on deck, had not been successful. The author also speculated that Germans off Great Britain were using wireless.

U.S. Navy World War I submarine missions occasioned many escapades of near disaster from hostile or near hostile action by friendly convoy and convoy escorts. Primarily as a result of lack of communications, four U. S. Navy submarines, N-3, N-4, O-4 and O-5, were inadvertently fired upon during the summer of 1918. Total disaster was only avoided at the last moment in each case.

The N-3, after being hit by fire from a British transport and taking water in the torpedo room, was nearly rammed by an American destroyer coming within 20 yards. As a result of the accidental skirmish, an unexploded British 7.5 inch shell was found in the submarine's forward superstructure.

The N-4, previously damaged by a collision, was fired upon by a British steamer while the submarine was slowly en route to New London.

Six days out of New York City, after completing convoy escort and inbound, the O-4 was fired upon by a convoy steamer; but the shots fell short. Identification was then successfully established. There were procedures for recognition in place, but positive identification and reliable ways to communicate were not available. Friendly force action against submarines also occurred during World War II.

A 1920 Naval Institute Proceedings article on American submarine operations during the War commented on World War I submarine N-5's radio communication posture. The N-5 was one of seven N class submarines constructed by the Electric Boat Company during 1917-18. During the last year of the war in order to receive radio communications the N-5 surfaced, raised the radio masts, and listened for further orders from the Navy shore radio stations at Arlington, Virginia (completed late in 1912) or at Siasconset on Nantucket off the coast of Massachusetts.

In the early post World War I period, the establishment of the Radio Corporation of America and the start of the Naval Research Laboratory at about the same time significantly impacted Navy radio communications growth and effectiveness.

In October 1919, RCA was founded by the General Electric Company and included holdings of the Marconi Wireless Telegraph Company of America, a subsidiary of a British-owned company. The Marconi Company owned Navy-leased wireless equipment both shore- and ship-based. This action provided a United States-based radio equipment manufacturing source for the Navy that would always remain under American control. Lessons from World War I regarding potential problems in the event of foreign monopoly of some segment of the wireless industry led the Navy to look favorably at such a corporation.

Further, by consent, RCA had legal access to a number of radio and related patents stemming from a variety of sources. In the early 1920s, in addition to General Electric, Westinghouse and American Telephone and Telegraph Company were the original shareholders of RCA. These three companies accounted for more than half of the stock holdings. Radio-related patents of the several companies were available to the new corporation.

Scientific American of April 1920 reported *Loop Aerials for Submarines.* The article was based on a paper read before the American Physical Society and reported some results of experiments made aboard a submarine to determine radio communications performance. This successful antenna concept is sometimes called the clearing line loop. The clearing lines, cables located over the submarine from bow to stern, were used to keep off debris and prevent damage to the submarine when surfacing. The loop attached to the clearing lines consisted of two insulated wires connected (grounded) to the submarine hull at the bow and the stern. It was carried over suitable supports to the bridge and then radio lead-ins to the receiving and transmitting apparatus. The submarine loop antenna outperformed ordinary antennas. The maximum depth of submergence for receiving was found to be frequency dependent. At radio frequencies of the order of 30 kHz, signals could be received when the top of the loop was submerged 21 feet. Transmitting from the loop at a frequency of about 300 kHz, distances of 10 or 12 miles were obtained when the top of the loop was practically at the surface. This range was found to decrease to two or three miles when the top of the loop was eight or nine feet below the surface. It was also noted that the loop could be used as a direction finder, maximum signals being received when the submarine was pointing toward the transmitting station. Limitations of the clearing line loop included obstruction of firing from the deck guns and easier detection of a surface submarine by enemy aircraft.

These findings indicated modest progress and a growing understanding of the submarine's needs and its environment. The requisite radio communication technologies making the submarine the ultimate war machine would only slowly evolve and begin to be available in the post World War II era and beyond.

The submarine's continuously broadening acceptance, increased numbers; propulsion enhancements, improved weapons and tactical value placed radio communications demands beyond the state-of-the-art available radio communication equipment.

The Naval Research Laboratory (NRL) Begins

Early in World War I, Germany's submarine effectiveness and the observed importance of science on warfare affirmed the need for a new Navy laboratory for experimental research, to be managed by civilians under the direction of a naval officer. In August 1916, an Act of Congress established and funded the new research laboratory under the direction of the Secretary of the Navy. NRL's charter included a vast number of technical areas including radio. Lack of agreement on the location of the laboratory and the United States' entrance into the war the following year delayed the construction of the laboratory until December 1920.

In early 1923, the first five buildings of NRL were completed. The site selected was at the Bellevue Arsenal on the Potomac River below Washington. They were augmented by addition of the Naval Aircraft Laboratory, the Naval Radio Telegraphic Laboratory, and the Radio Test Shop from the Washington Navy Yard.

Some of the areas of NRL's work which contributed in the effectiveness of submarine radio communications during the period between World War I and World War II included radio propagation studies, the Navy's adoption of high frequencies (HF), high frequency equipment, intrafleet HF equipment, crystal frequency control, and submarine HF transmitters.

By 1924, the growing needs for commercial radio broadcasting led to the establishment of the broadcast band, 550-1550 kHz. Between 1900-1920, the Navy primarily used radio frequencies below 600 kHz; but the Navy had plans to use what became the broadcast band for future intrafleet communications. This development led the Navy to consider frequencies above the broadcast band. Building on the experience of the radio amateurs who from 1912 had access to frequencies above 1500 kHz, NRL examined this part of the spectrum and developed propagation theory to predict performance at the high frequencies. For long range communications, HF provided improved performance. The equipment required less power and was more compact and lighter. The equipment cost was relatively lower; and, further, more channels were available to the Navy.

Interest in HF was further increased because the new Navy fleet organization made in 1922 created a need for more channels for radio circuits between the various fleet elements. Multiple frequency reception and transmission from the ships was also a requirement for consideration.

After several years of HF propagation studies, equipment development, and various experiments and tests, a definitive long range round-the-world HF test was conducted in 1926. Successful extensive long distance tests at HF were held between NRL and the *USS Seattle* operating in Melbourne, Australia. In late 1926 the Navy decided to include HF equipment in its Radio Modernization Plan, then undergoing revision. Planned HF installations were greatly extended beyond the earlier recommendations.

The Navy's use of HF (2,000 to 18,100 kHz) made possible antennas smaller in size and reasonably compatible with the spaces available on a submarine. Further in 1927-28, NRL developed a new HF transmitter for submarine use.

To demonstrate the HF capability, two fleet submarines (V-1 and V-2), commissioned in 1924), had the new transmitters and antennas installed in June 1928 at San Francisco. The submarines conducted transmit and receive tests in the Pacific. They were able to communicate both day and night with NRL in Washington, DC, from Hawaii. At the time, this was a long distance communication record for a submarine.

Other United States submarines were smaller than the larger V class and could not accommodate the HF transmitter. Therefore, in the following year (1929) NRL developed a second HF submarine transmitter suited to the smaller space available on the non-fleet type submarines.

This new submarine transmitter was made in sections to fit the limitations of submarine hatch diameters and passageway constraints of the S class. Using higher radio frequencies (shorter wavelengths) also made it possible to use several different antenna configurations which were less constraining than the antenna needs for the previously-used lower frequencies. In particular, the success of HF made it possible to eliminate the cumbersome clearing line loop previously mentioned. Loop, flat top, and periscope-mounted antennas could be used with these new NRL transmitters.

November 1929 submarine patrol trials with the new NRL HF transmitters proved successful, establishing a HF range capability of about 575 miles. Under various limited and constrained conditions of submarine operating depth, ranges of the order of 90 miles were achieved.

During 1930 and 1932, 20 of NRL's LF/HF transmitters were procured from industry. They were for use on some of the S class coastal submarines which operated with the V class submarines. Additional production of submarine transmitters occurred in 1933 and 1935. In the period 1930-45, leading up to and including World War II, various versions of NRL's transmitters provided the foundation for both the shipboard and shore station transmitters.

By 1930, submarine HF communications proved to be useful for scouting and screening submarines in support of the fleet. It was noted that submarines could be maneuvered by radio in a way not unlike visual communications.

To support the HF transmitters, NRL developed a tuned radio frequency HF receiver in the mid-1920s. A commercial procurement made the receiver available to various ships, shore stations, the Marine Corps, and the U. S.

Coast Guard. A later receiver was produced in quantity (about 1000) and provided throughout the naval service.

By 1934, NRL's work toward developing a suitable Navy HF superheterodyne receiver resulted in commercial procurement. This series of receivers was purchased in large numbers during World War II.

In 1940, after four decades of radio development, submarine communications had improved, but with continuing limitations. At the beginning of World War II, the submarine could receive messages at long ranges of thousands of miles with dependable very low frequency (VLF) one way link to shore. Messages were sent via the VLF Fox method developed in 1914 during World War I, a no receipt transmission from a shore station on a four-hour schedule with repeated messages to ensure reception. The submarine posture for reception was at that time typically at periscope depth with a loop receiving antenna aligned with the distant VLF transmitter. Receiving posture could require as long as an hour. Another factor in the time equation for message reception was the sea state and its impact on the submarine.

HF transmission and reception for the submarine was the other primary channel. At HF, an important adverse consideration during transmission was the vulnerability of the submarine from enemy direction-finding techniques. These frequencies also required operation at periscope depth, a constraint similar to that of VLF.

Communication, an essential part of submarine operation, therefore presented a high risk aspect which had to be balanced with the submarine's purpose or mission and its safety.

As the intensity of World War II deepened in 1940, the typical submarine was vastly different than Holland's 53 foot long craft with a crew of nine, a bow torpedo tube and three torpedoes. The wartime fleet type submarine was 300 feet long and had a cruising range of 11,000 miles. A crew of about 80 was average. Radio communication equipment, although not perfectly matched to this submarine much advanced from Holland's designs, did meet the needs of the time.

After World War II

Both ends of the electromagnetic spectrum were exploited to enhance submarine communications after World War II. Satellites, computers, and other new knowledge during the next half century alleviated some of the needs. But the oceans above and below the submarine do not easily submit to the submarine's communication needs.

Bibliography

Alden, John D., The Fleet Submarine in the U. S. Navy – Design and Construction History, Annapolis: Naval Institute Press, 1979.

Bilby, Kenneth, General David Sarnoff and the Rise of the Communication Industry. New York: Harper and Row, 1986.

Bridge, Admiral Sir Cyprian, The Art of Naval Warfare: Introductory Observations. London: Smith Elder and Company, 1907.

Compton-Hall, Richard, The Underwater War: 1939-1945. Branford Press, 1982.

---------, Submarine Boats, the Beginning of Underwater Warfare. New York: Arco Publishing, 1983.

---------, Submarine versus Submarine. New York: Orion Books, 1988.

---------, Submarines and the War at Sea 1914-1918. London: Macmillan, 1991.

Friedman, Norman, Submarine Design and Development. Annapolis: Naval Institute Press, 1984.

Gebbard, Louis A., Evolution of Naval Radio-Electronics and Contributions of the Naval Research Laboratory. NRL Report 8300. Washington: Government Printing Office, 1979.

Gray, Edwyn, The Underwater War Submarines: 1914-1918. New York: Charles Scribner's Sons, 1971.

---------, The Devil's Device: Robert Whitehead and the History of the Torpedo. Revised and Updated Edition, Annapolis: Naval Institute, 1991.

Leinwall, Stanley, From Spark to Satellite: A History of Radio Communication. New York: Charles Scribner's Sons, 1979.

Marconi, Degna, My Father Marconi. New York: McGraw Hill, 1962.

Morris, Richard K. John P. Holland 1841-1914: Inventor of the Modern Submarine. Annapolis: U.S. Naval Institute, 1966.

Weir, Gary E., Forged in War—The Naval Industrial Complex and American Submarine Construction. Washington: Naval Historical Center, 1993.

FLOATING WIRE ANTENNAS COMMUNICATING WITH SUBMERGED SUBMARINES

The concept of a floating wire antenna for submarines arrived on the Navy's communication horizon in 1954, the same year as the launching and commissioning of the first nuclear submarine *USS Nautilus* (SSN 571). Six years later, in 1960, *USS Triton* (SSNR 586) was able to deploy a buoyant cable antenna and maintain continuous radio reception during its historic circumnavigation of the world while submerged. From its beginnings, the floating wire antenna has provided capabilities which have steadily improved and reflected the communication needs of nuclear submarine platforms.

In the mid 1950s, interest in this type of antenna at the Navy Underwater Sound Laboratory[1] in New London was directed to the communication requirements of the diesel submarine while submerged. During the early years, research worked with this antenna toward providing the submerged submarine a send-and-receive capability. The frequencies of interest were 2 to 30 x 10^6 Hz. At that time, submarines periodically still rose to, or neared, the surface to charge batteries and conduct radio frequency communications.

----

[1] Excellent guidance was provided to the author by Anthony Susi, the Laboratory's long-term buoyant cable antenna manager. Susi's involvement with buoyant cable antennas on both national and international levels covers more than 30 years.

Nautilus, a true submersible with the ability to spend extensive periods submerged, provided additional submarine antenna challenges including new speed and depth considerations. As the nuclear submarine program grew, each new class of attack and fleet ballistic missile submarine brought fresh, interesting, and difficult challenges to the Underwater Sound Laboratory (USL) antenna engineers, scientists and technicians.

Technology, patience, support and hard work gave a viable buoyant cable antenna to attack and strategic submarines by the mid-1960s. Today, an inboard retrievable buoyant cable antenna is part of the antenna suite of all U. S. submarines and those of major foreign powers.

James Tennyson

Introduction of this submarine antenna concept resulted from the initiatives and investigations of James Tennyson, a physicist and inventor working in the Radio Communications Branch of the Electromagnetics Division of USL. He came to the New London Laboratory from the Naval Research Laboratory in February 1947 when the submarine radio research group was still in a formative stage.

Beginnings

In October 1944, during World War II, a German conference was held on underwater antennas in Berlin. Minutes of this wartime conference mentioned the possible use of a floating cable antenna towed by submarine for radio communications. The report of the conference came to the attention of Tennyson in the early 1950s. The idea caught his interest. After some preliminary research and limited encouragement, he proceeded with development of an experimental floating wire antenna. The initial thrust was to use a floating wire to address the problem of intra-fleet communications. An early goal was to provide a range in the order of 20 miles.

First problems included how to make an antenna that would float. This was one of the tasks that John Amaral, a long time radio engineer at the Laboratory, helped to resolve. He assisted Tennyson in all the early experiments and at-sea tests. At the Laboratory he fabricated the first antennas that would float. His installations and tests of these early floating wire antennas included the submarines *Barracuda* (SST 3), *Bonita* (SS 551) and *Bass* (SS 552), [Editor's Note: *Barracuda* was redesignated from SSK 1 to SST3 in July 1959. *Bass* and *Bonita* were redesignated from SSK2 and SSK3 to SS 551 and SS 552 respectively in December 1955] as well as others. One early sea test with floating wire antennas involved Amaral in an under-the-ice exercise in he North Atlantic involving three diesel submarines and at-sea transfer from one submarine to another in polynya.

The Antenna

Initial laboratory investigations into the capability of an antenna to radiate while floating just above seawater were conducted at the USL test facility located at Fishers Island, New York, six miles from the New London Laboratory. An underground laboratory below a 50-foot diameter ground level seawater test pool allowed measurements to be made on antennas placed in the pool simulating the condition of a submerged submarine.

The first floating wire antennas, as previously mentioned, were made at the Laboratory. A 100-foot length of a standard coaxial cable (RG-14/U) was used. Flotation was achieved by using 50 small football-shaped fishnet floats six inches long and three inches in diameter along the cable. The outer jacket and metal braid were stripped from the last 25 feet of the cable.[2] Floating on the surface, this 25-foot length of center conductor separated from the seawater by the cable's dielectric became the active part of the antenna. For the next several years, this was the basic design.

In July 1954, Tennyson and Amaral conducted a successful at-sea test with the experimental antenna on the submarine *USS Tusk* (SS 426). The first communication was between *Tusk* and the laboratory site on Fishers Island, New York. As mentioned, the interest was in transmitting and receiving while submerged. Later in 1962 and 1964, Tennyson was awarded patents for floating wire antenna invention.

The early antennas with floats were about 100 feet long. The lead-in end was attached to an antenna fitting on the sail while the outboard end was always made so that the antenna could not reach and tangle in the screw. The original antennas were throw-over-the-side wires with floats.

The concept was a success. However, during the following years both difficult and first-ever technological challenges were continuously addressed. Antenna frequency considerations, how to make an antenna that would be buoyant without the fish net floats, and how to have an overall antenna system compatible with the submarine's requirements were some of the problems that lay beyond this first demonstration on *Tusk*.

----

[2] Early laboratory experiments used cables placed on wooden 2x10 inch planks for flotation.
Later, when submarine-tested early antennas were returned to the Laboratory, the football shaped floats were found to be much reduced in size due to the pressure at the depths where the antenna had been towed.

First Buoyant Cable

In 1956, further development of the antenna at USL was transferred to the Antenna Branch of the Laboratory's Electromagnetic Division. An RF cable for the antenna that would have buoyancy and not require floats was sought, and the first length of cable was delivered by a cable company in 1958. Obtaining the sufficient buoyancy, cable strength, and ease of handling the cable were some of the many antenna requirements which had to be met. Between 1959 and 1969, with the cooperation of many cable manufacturers, USL developed approximately 36 different versions of single conductor and coaxial buoyant cable.

USL antenna engineers Warner Adams and Richard Jones developed the first mechanized system. In August 1958, it was tested at sea onboard *USS Barracuda*. This system was the inaugural use of an inherently buoyant cable with a cable payout and retrieval reel (on the afterdeck of *Barracuda*). It was also the first time that up to 1000 feet of cable could be streamed, allowing the submarine to communicate at deeper depths. COMSUBLANT reported that viable submarine-aircraft and submarine-surface ship communication ranges were achieved from a submerged submarine. The external reel system arrangement was overtaken by further developments which provided an inboard launching and recovery of the buoyant cable.

RF Reception Below Periscope Depth

Emphasis in succeeding years was on developing the buoyant cable antenna concept to meet the operational requirement for VLF and LF reception below periscope depth. Developing an antenna compatible with the nuclear submarine's changing speed and depth requirements was elusive, at least initially.

However, by the end of the 1950s, USL was manufacturing fixed-length buoyant cable antenna installations which provided submerged reception on a number of landmark submarine missions.

In 1959, *USS Skate* (SSN 578), using an early one-inch diameter buoyant cable antenna received broadcast under the Arctic icecap while making a North Pole transit. (The previous year, *Nautilus* was the first submarine to make the transit.) The following year, 1960, *USS Triton*, using a smaller diameter (5/8- inch) buoyant cable antenna, maintained continuous radio reception during the previously cited historic circumnavigation of the world while sub-merged. The antenna was streamed throughout the entire trip without mishap or failure. The first fleet ballistic missile submarine, *USS George Washington* (SSBN 598), successfully used a fixed-length outboard-connected type buoyant cable antenna during an early patrol (1960) and reliably received VLF broadcasts while remaining completely submerged.

The fixed-length outboard-connected type limited submarine operability when using the antenna. In order to receive, the several-hundred-foot antenna restricted the submarine's speed and depth. Further, if the antenna was damaged or cut, the submarine would have to surface to replace or repair it since the antenna was not inboard retrievable.

Antenna Inboard Retrievability Demonstration

In 1960, U.S. Navy Commander (later Captain) Arthur P. Sibold Jr., during his assignment as Senior Program Officer and Executive Officer on the staff of the Commanding Officer and Director of USL, investigated the inboard recoverability problem and identified an innovative solution. At this time, USL was heavily involved in several aspects of Polaris submarine communications, including both electromagnetic and acoustic.

He proposed the idea of using a line wiper of the type found in the oil drilling industry to pay out and reel in the USL-developed floating wire antenna from inside the submarine. He conducted a test in June 1960 onboard *USS Hardhead* (SS 365) off New London. The line wiper was developed in the mid- 1950s by Bowen-Itco in conjunction with paraffin removal in oil well operations under presssure. The test was successful in demonstrating that a floating wire antenna could be paid in and out and retrieved from inside the submarine.

On 3 June 1960, Commander Sibold wrote a USNUSL Technical Memorandum outlining his design concept, *Recommended Approach to Development of a Recoverable Floating Wire Antenna*. This was followed by an 8 June 1960 Technical Memorandum, *Report of Test of Recoverable Floating Wire Antenna*, which reports the sea test results.

In 1964, Commander Sibold filed for a patent on his invention and was granted a patent for a Pressure-Proof Hull Fitting on April 2, 1966. The patent addressed providing the submarine with the capability of launching, repairing and recovering of devices such as a VLF communications antenna towed astern while the submarine is underway and submerged.

Inboard Retrievable Buoyant Cable Antenna Systems

Tennyson's invention brought about practical reception of RF signals below periscope depth. The nuclear submarine brought with it the necessity of receiving while submerged. The Polaris program increased the requirements for submarine communications. New speed and depth needs as the new nuclear classes evolved kept increasing the

39

challenge. Commander Sibold's demonstration pointed the way to provide an antenna system which could be brought inside the submarine for repair, replacement or stowage while the submarine was underway and submerged.

The device. called a transfer mechanism, to accomplish the inboard handling of buoyant cables hundreds of feet in length led to an evolutionary research and development program; and in the early 1970s, a standard transfer mechanism was available (BRA-24).

Like all submarine antennas, buoyant cable antennas confront extreme temperatures, high pressure, severe drag forces and high sea states. In addition, buoyant cable antennas accommodate the transfer mechanism and are wound and unwound from a drum. Mechanical requirements are measured in thousands of pounds of pull. Further, the antenna had to meet the radio frequency specifications.

Between 1959 and 1989, a series of ten developmental antennas were produced, most of which were configured with a 0.65-inch-diameter antenna which has become the standard size. The antennas had steadily increasing break strength of 1000 pounds in 1950 and finally as much as 5000 pounds in some current designs. It was the advent of the commercial production of Kevlar as an antenna strength member that brought about the enhanced break numbers. The results of these improvements is seen in the speed/depth performance curves of these carefully designed and produced antennas.

In general, buoyant cable antenna effectiveness was improved by in-line electronic miniaturization, materials developments, and other advanced techniques. Over several decades, the realization of better cables, active in-line amplification at the antenna element, design and development of improved connectors compatible with the transfer mechanism and other devices led to a series of patents to various Laboratory personnel: A. Susi, L. Carnaghan, R. Phillips, and B. Pease.

ELF and the Floating Wire Antenna

In 1963, under the broad Polaris Special Project Program called Pangloss, extensive efforts were being made to address a solution to communicating from land to submerged submarines. At that time, extremely low frequency (ELF) was an experimental candidate to satisfy the Navy's need for secure radio wave transmission to submerged fleet ballistic missile submarines.

An intensive six weeks of communication tests were made starting January 21,1963 with a receiver installed on *USS Seawolf* (SSN 575). At that time, the experimental ELF transmitter was located in North Carolina and the transmitting antenna was 109 miles long, oriented north-easterly. The submarine was equipped with a 1000-foot trailing wire antenna, at the end of which was a pair of sensors. Signals in the ELF spectrum were measured at ranges of about 2000 miles in the North Atlantic with the trailing wire at keel depth. At greater depths, signals were received at a range of more than 500 miles with the antenna. ELF permitted reception at antenna depths much greater than was possible with VLF. The tests on *Seawolf* using a floating wire antenna supported the feasibility of ELF reception by a submarine at operational depths.

These communication tests established that a deployed submarine could receive messages from the continental United States without severe reductions in the submarine's operational capability during reception. This was a *first* in the history of submarine communications.

During the extensive at-sea testing conducted over a number of years during the development and implementation of ELF, the Laboratory's buoyant cable was a key element of the submarine suite. For example, a successful ELF communication test was conducted in 1976, using a floating wire antenna, on a submarine traveling at 16 knots at a depth of 427 feet under 33 feet of Arctic sea ice. The Wisconsin ELF test facility was the signal source.[3]

Summing Up

Submerged reception at operational speeds and depths at frequencies in the order of tens of Hertz to the Megahertz region are the result of 50 years of hands-on effort at the New London Laboratory. Support by the Navy in Washington and a multiplicity of sea tests on diesel and all classes of nuclear submarines at locations around the globe brought Tennyson's vision to a firm reality and a submarine antenna capability will improve further in the future

---

[3] The operational transfer of the ELF communications system from Commander, Space and Naval Warfare Systems Command, to Commander, Naval Telecommunications Command, took place in October 1989. The buoyant cable antenna has always been a pivotal element in the successful performance of the ELF communication system.

New London Public Library Archives

USS George Washington (SSBN 598)
(Underwater Sound Laboratory in background)

Courtesy Submarine Force Library and Museum

SS Seawolf (SSN 575) ELF Communication Tests 1963
SS Nautilus (SSN 571 in background

APRIL 1900: INVENTOR-BUILDER JOHN P. HOLLAND DELIVERS FIRST U.S. SUBMARINE

Part One

As the new century began, John P. Holland (submarine builder and inventor whose concepts revolutionized naval warfare) was nearing the pinnacle of his success with the United States Navy purchasing his successful submarine *Holland VI.*

Holland descended gradually from this high point of his career. It had taken Holland 25 years and the construction of five submarines to arrive at his current design of a practical submarine. True recognition of his accomplishment was not realized until after his death in 1914.

At this time Theodore Roosevelt (former Assistant Secretary of the Navy and strongly favorable for a better Navy) was concluding his governance of New York State and within months of his presidency (1901-1909), and American submarine builders were embarking on a century-long development of the submarine as a significant weapon.

In 1899, the recently-incorporated Electric Boat Company (EBCO) included the Holland Torpedo Boat Company in its acquisitions. EBCO provided needed fiscal and business support to Holland during the final pre-delivery stages of the three years of intensive testing, modifying and establishing the value of Holland VI to the Navy and others. EBCO went on to become one of the world's foremost builders of submarines, by 1995 delivering more than 260 submarines to the Navy. The EBCO sale of a $150,000 submarine in 1900 was a modest beginning for a 20th Century military/industrial relationship of enormous importance.

President Roosevelt's international ambitions and the need for a growing modern Navy provided impetus to acceptance of the fledgling submarine. Holland's successful submarine provided the starting point of what became the American submarine industry with the essential ingredients of private profit motivation and industrial know-how. Also it took on an international flavor, thrusting the submarine into prominence both at home and abroad.

The submarine represented the increasing trend toward the use of new and more complex technologies for sophisticated armament. The research, development and fabrication for the new approach to armament was often beyond government abilities. In procuring technical armament, institutional experience for buyers such as the Navy during procurement became an essential requirement. Then and in the years ahead this was not always available; sometimes this created awkward consequences.

Roosevelt's enterprising role and experience as Assistant Secretary of the Navy (1897-1889) made for an opportune time to bring the submarine in as an addition to the Navy's growing arsenal. On April 10, 1898, while *Holland VI* was undergoing its long testing and acceptance program, he wrote to the then Secretary of the Navy John D. Long (1897-1902):

"I think that the Holland submarine boat should be purchased. Evidently she has in her great possibilities for harbor defense. Sometimes she

46

doesn't work perfectly, but often she does, and I don't think that in the present emergency we can afford to let her slip. I recommend that you authorize me to enter into negotiations for her, or that you authorize the Bureau of Construction to do so, which would be just as well."[1]

The Navy's 1900 purchase of a submarine was more than the end product of naval contracts and culmination of a quarter century's intensive effort by a motivated and talented Irish immigrant, John Holland. The beginnings of the tangle of circumstances which brought to fruition this then world class submarine resulted both from the determination of the country and the Navy to grow nationally and internationally and in Holland's resolve to build the right submarine.

In 1878, Secretary of the Navy Richard Thompson (1877-1881) was told of the minimal size of the current serviceable Navy (33 cruisers, 13 monitors, and two gunboats). This marginal fleet placed the United States Navy 12th worldwide in ironclad strength below Chile. The next 20 years saw the Presidents, Congress and general public favorable toward developing a larger and better Navy. As the Navy's needs were gradually fulfilled, the collected efforts became identified with the expression *New Navy* or *Steel Navy.*

President Grover Cleveland's Secretary of the Navy, New York lawyer and businessman, William Collins Whitney (1885-1889), observed on the day he took office that "the United States Navy had no one vessel of war which could have kept the seas open for one week as against any

---

[1] John Niven et al., <u>Dynamic America</u>. General Dynamics with Doubleday, n.d., p. 69.

first rate naval power."[2] The Navy's ships were still mostly wood with a few obsolete ironclads.

In 1898, by the end of the 100-day war with Spain, United States naval successes reflected the beginnings of that New Navy, standing sixth in the world. The end of Theodore Roosevelt's second presidential term saw a growing Navy ranking second or third in the world. Submarines comprised a small part of the Navy's modernization and growth, which focused on battleships, an isthmian canal, and possession of Hawaii.

Acceptance of the submarine was slow but unlike the acceptance of steam power over sail which required decades. In 1900, with centuries of surface ship tradition, priority and budgetary decisions of the predominately surface ship officer corps did not particularly favor the infant submarine technology and an energetic exploitation of the submarine's tactical and strategic potentials. A further impediment for submarine acceptance was the torpedo boat, acknowledged as the mainstay of coast defense. Further, torpedo boats were not excessively expensive and could be built in a few months. Roosevelt, as Assistant Secretary of the Navy, ordered 75 to be constructed.

Prior to 1900 and United States' purchase of *Holland VI*, France was the only nation to have a submarine fleet. In 1863, a not-too-successful French submarine, 140 feet long, *Le Plongeur,* was in operation. The French Navy continued to encourage French designers and by 1886 began ordering large numbers of submarines, expending government resources for a particular strategic need. Further, France saw the submarine's offensive as well as defensive value and regarded the submarine as a safeguard against an attacking

---

[2] Robert Kanigel, The One Best Way: Frederick Winslow Taylor and the Enigma of Efficiency, Viking, New York, 1997, p. 241.

British Navy in the event of war.[3] By 1880, there were 42 separate submarine projects under way in various nations, 15 of which led to finished boats.[4]

The French and international view of the submarine as a coastal defense weapon remained entrenched until World War I, when Germany's successful submarines destroyed naval as well as merchant ships in an unforeseen offensive role.

John Holland

To describe Holland, words such as visionary, persevering, gifted, insightful, daring, and hardworking seem appropriate. Born on the coast of Ireland in 1841, Holland lived his early life in very limited circumstances. Early, he demonstrated aptitude for physical sciences but was restricted in vocational directions by poor health, nearsightedness, and lack of funds. At 17, in 1858, he joined the Irish Christian Brothers, a teaching order, becoming a teacher. Under the Brothers' tutelage his mechanical aptitude, drafting skill and mathematical abilities developed.

As a child witness of the Irish famine (1846-51), Holland saw his father, uncles and male relatives succumbing to hardships and disease (possibly Asiatic cholera). Further, he would have been aware of the spectacle of mass emigration primarily to America as a result of the famine and general economic conditions.

In his later teen years, it is probable that Holland's views of his homeland were also influenced by the ongoing political turmoil related to Ireland's desire for independence in which his brothers were involved. His younger brother, an active member of the secret Fenian society established in

[3] New York Times, January 20, 1900, p.4.
[4] Clay Blair, Jr., Silent Victory; The U.S. Submarine War Against Japan, J.B. Lippincott Company, Philadelphia and New York 1975, p. 26.

Ireland in 1858 to challenge English rule, found it desirable to leave for American in 1869. In the years ahead, the Fenians played a decisive role in Holland's submarine-inventing and -building career.

Holland's mother and older brother left Ireland for America in early 1872. With few ties remaining in Ireland, Holland withdrew from the Christian Brothers and took steerage passage to Boston, landing in November 1873.

Shortly after arrival, he slipped on the ice, broke his leg and spent time convalescing. Later, in an interview with the *Washington Star* in 1900, he recalled that during his recovery he reconsidered his earlier thoughts on basic problems of submarine navigation. In 1874, he was again teaching with the Christian Brothers, this time in Paterson, New Jersey.

Holland's Six Submarines (1878-1900) [5]

In addition to teaching, Holland developed plans for an original one-man submarine. He found investors to support him in the event that he could obtain a government endorsement. In 1875, he submitted his plan for a 14-foot submarine to President Grant's Secretary of the Navy George M. Robeson (1869-1877). The Navy's reply agreed technically with Holland but did not believe that anyone could be convinced to operate the submarine underwater.

Private submarine building occupied Holland for the following ten years. As engineer and innovator with hands-on direction and experience, he launched three submarines: *Holland I* in May 1878, *Fenian Ram* in May 1881, and *Fenian Model* in November 1883. Fenian Society activists in the New York area provided the funding, intending that these submarines would be transported to Europe and used to

---

[5] Richard K. Morris, John P. Holland: 1841-1914 Inventor of the Modern Submarine, United States Naval Institute, Annapolis MD, 1966, p. 175.

inflict damage on the British fleet. It is important to note that these Fenian boats were equipped with Brayton internal combustion engines and not the steam that was in vogue. The boats met specifications, but none found its way beyond the New York area for the intended purpose.

Two years later in 1885, based on Holland's designs and efforts at the Nautilus Submarine Boat Company, the privately-financed 50-foot wood and steel Zalinski Boat was launched. During launching, the submarine was critically damaged and later discarded. This disaster temporarily brought Holland's submarine development efforts to a standstill. At that time, he held several submarine-related patents.

In 1888, with encouragement by naval officers and Secretary of the Navy Whitney, Congress appropriated $150,000 for a submarine. Whitney invited submarine developers to submit their designs and competitive bids. Holland's design, reviewed with those of five other competitors from the United States and overseas, won. The government then cancelled the plans for submarine procurement. The following year, there was a second call for bids. Holland's design again triumphed, and Secretary of the Navy Benjamin Franklin Tracy (1889-1893) reallocated the submarine funds to complete surface ships.

During this period of turndowns by the Navy, Holland obtained a position with Morris and Cummings Dredging Company as an equipment designer. While with Morris until 1893, Holland made the acquaintance of a company lawyer, Elihu B. Frost.

Initially this was fortuitous for Holland. Naval historian Albert B. Christman, in writing about Holland commented concerning Frost that "Besides knowing the law Frost had Washington connections, a keen sense of business and politics, and uncommon admiration for John Holland's technical skill and determination."[6]

As a result of Frost's efforts, energy, and enthusiasm, early in 1893 the John P. Holland Torpedo Boat Company was formed, incorporated in New York State, and stock issued. Holland became the company manager. Holland then held United States patents for "a gun patent, a steering apparatus for submarine vessels (patented early in 1893), and another submarine design for which a patent was still pending."[7]

Because of the Navy's reluctance to move forward with submarine construction, Frost took action abroad to obtain foreign patents for Holland's designs. Patent sales were sought in European capitals, Japan, and the South American countries of Peru, Chile, Ecuador, and Argentina. Sales of Holland's patents to foreign nations potentially provided opportunity for submarine building abroad while the United States Navy procrastinated. Later foreign patents played a formidable role in Holland's demise as a submarine builder.

Congress appropriated $200,000 in March 1893 to reopen design competition for an experimental submarine. April brought a call for submarine design. For the fifth time Holland submitted his submarine plans; and when the bids were opened June 30, Holland again was first. Supporters favoring construction of the submarine included President Grover Cleveland. However, others in the Washington bureaucracy stalled award of the contract.

To justify a technical question regarding submarine habitability, an experiment was conducted at Newport, RI in which a cat, a rooster, a rabbit, and a dove were submerged

[6] Albert B. Christman, Naval Innovators: 1776-1900, Naval Surface Warfare Center, Dahlgren, VA, August 1989, p. 346.
[7] Morris, op. cit., p. 65.

in a watertight metal container. Explosions of gunpowder were made increasingly closer to the container, each with a larger charge and finally, at 30 yards distance, 100 pounds of gunpowder. The cat and the rooster survived. The metal container was not damaged, yet the favorable test results did not fully convince all who were concerned.

Pro-Holland efforts to obtain the release of the Congressionally-appropriated funds by convincing Navy Boards, Senators, the Secretary of the Navy and others were successful. Finally, almost two years later on March 3, 1895, Frost gained the $200,000 contract. This incessant assault on the bureaucracy was an essential ingredient in obtaining the contract. This was seven years after the first naval competition for submarine design and 20 years from Holland's first approach to the Navy with a submarine design.

The position of the Navy with regard to the implementation of the new submarine contract has been inferred by some as being adversarial. Another author saw the Navy's attitude as "The navy had lost the war, but it remained resolute in its determination to be anything but cooperative in defeat."[8]

At the Columbia Iron Works in Baltimore, the scene of the new construction opened with a keel laying in 1896 for the new submarine called *Plunger*. Even at the start, design concepts were put in place contrary to Holland's experience and design. Two of his previous submarines were propelled on the surface using the Brayton internal combustion petroleum engine with a single propeller. The 85-foot *Plunger* required a 1500 hp engine to obtain the specified speed on the surface.

---

[8] Christman, op. cit., p. 346.

Steam was the only viable way to meet the substantial horsepower requirement, yet steam had already been shown to be impractical by European submarine builders. On *Plunger*, engine heat in the fireroom at 130 degrees F. made it extremely difficult for the crew. The specifications for the new submarine called for five propellers, three for forward motion and two that (it was hoped) would allow the boat to hover at fixed depths. These issues alone can be described as anti-Holland.

During *Plunger* construction, differences between Holland and onsite Navy personal continued. Holland's decades of experience included design, construction, and operation of four submarines. Involved Navy personnel proved limited in submarine knowledge and oriented to conventional shipbuilding. A fully maneuverable submarine with ease of submerging and surfacing similar to a dolphin's performance was dominant in Holland's operating requirements. The Holland hull configuration would be fishlike, not that of a surface craft.

The *Plunger* design was moving in directions not in tune with Holland's concept. The continuing flow of changes by the Navy made construction difficult and tended to make *Plunger* look more like a surface vessel, contrary to Holland's goal of a hull design enhancing underwater maneuverability.

Launched in 1897 with unresolved technical problems, *Plunger* did not get beyond dock trials at the Iron Works. Steam propulsion and its difficulties were overtaken by internal combustion engine advances. The same year, the Otto engine, a new internal combustion petroleum-operated engine, was acclaimed at an international exhibition in Paris. The horsepower was adequate for submarine surface operation for a smaller submarine. Holland was aware of this development.

Prior to the launching of *Plunger*, Holland initiated a parallel submarine enterprise in adjacent New Jersey at Lewis Nixon's Crescent Shipyard in Elizabethport, to build with private funds a smaller submarine of his design, incorporating the latest technology, a 45 hp Otto engine, and without interference from the Navy. The new submarine, *Holland VI*, at 54 feet in length was more than 30 feet shorter than the 85- foot *Plunger* with its 1500-hp steam engine requirement. Almost four years later in April 1900, the Navy purchased its first submarine, *Holland VI*.

APRIL 1900: INVENTOR-BUILDER JOHN P. HOLLAND DELIVERS FIRST U.S. SUBMARINE

Part Two

HOLLAND VI

Early on, Holland perceived the problem related to building *Plunger* and the growing conflicts with the Navy's oversight. With difficulty, private financial support (a gift by Mrs. Isaac Lawrence of New York) was found for construction of Holland's sixth submarine in parallel with the ongoing construction of the Navy- sponsored *Plunger*. It turned out that the new submarine *Holland VI* was launched in May 1897, several months ahead of *Plunger*.

Not without difficulties and several near tragedies, *Holland VI* became a reality and was the first underwater craft successfully to combine two means of propulsion: one for the surface, the other for running submerged. Holland's design with the more efficient Otto engine for surface operation allowed for recharging the batteries used for underwater running. Outstanding operating features included longitudinal stability, quick submergence, enhanced hydro-dynamic hull design, and a single torpedo tube and a dynamite gun that could be fired when either awash or submerged.[1]

After the launching, tests of submerging capabilities were met, adjustments made, and a successful dive achieved on St. Patrick's Day, March 17, 1898. Performance both underwater and at sea in open water demonstrated the boat's uniqueness and its fulfillment of Holland's design expectations. Frost brought his media skills to bear, (Elihu B. Frost, a lawyer with the Morris & Cummings Dredging Company with whom Holland was affiliated until 1893; see Part I in The Submarine Review, July 1998) and *Holland VI* was brought to the attention of the public.

It was at this juncture that Roosevelt, then Assistant Secretary of the Navy, made his previously-cited recommendation for the Navy to negotiate purchase of *Holland VI*.

By the summer of 1898, the submarine had been through some of its initial tests. A long underwater demonstration exceeded the requirements levied on *Plunger*. The need for some extensive modifications to the stern structure were identified. The Holland Company now required additional fiscal support for these alterations and to defray the cost of more submarine demonstrations for additional Navy scrutiny and convincing. These difficulties and others led Holland to his often-quoted comment, "What will the Navy require next? That my boat should be able to climb a tree?"

Isaac L. Rice, a Bavarian émigré and well known successful lawyer and financier, was president of the Electric Storage Battery Company of Philadelphia which provided batteries for *Holland VI*. After a demonstration ride during

---

[1] Richard K. Morris, "John P. Holland: Mechanical Genius." The Submarine Review, January 1998.

the summer on the new submarine, Rice became interested in forming a company to build submarines.

Rice brought his organizational skills and knowledge, including that of an authority in patent law, to the new submarine company and in February 1899 incorporated the Electric Boat Company on the foundations of the acquired Holland Torpedo Boat Company. Needed funds for the modifications to the submarine prior to the Navy's further testing were now available. The necessary exposure and publicity to convince the Navy to purchase were developed through the skills of both Rice and Frost.

The remodeling of *Holland VI* was completed towards the end of March 1899. On 25 March, Holland left for Europe on a combination business and pleasure trip. Near the time of his departure, the Company's secretary, Frost, paid five years of back taxes on all of Holland's foreign patents--British, German, Swedish and Belgian.[2] This lien on his patents ultimately contributed to Holland's separation in 1904 from the Electric Boat company, when he formally resigned. Regarding Holland's patents, Christman noted "Frost and others gained control of Holland's foreign patents and had many of his domestic patents assigned to the Electric Boat Company."[3]

In May 1899 the waters off Greenport, Long Island, were selected as a submarine testing site free from heavy water traffic and testing was resumed. Newspapers, weekly periodicals, and reports of rides on the submarine by the press, personnel of foreign navies and friends kept *Holland VI* in the limelight. One of the prominent riders was Clara Barton, founder of the American Red Cross. She was the first woman to be on board while the submarine submerged.

---

[2] Richard K. Morris, John P. Holland: 181-1914 Inventor of the Modern Submarine. United States Naval Institute, Annapolis MD, 1966, p. 99.
[3] Albert B. Christman, Naval Innovators:1776-1900, Naval Surface Warfare Center, Dahlgren, VA, August 1989, p. 350.

One of the tests off Long Island included a four- hour-long run which met with approval of the current Naval Board.

The submarine's performance was successful, but sale to the Navy had not been made. In the opinion of both Rice and Frost, each of whom possessed excellent lobbying skills, the best way to sell the submarine was to take it to Washington. This was accomplished by slowly towing the submarine to Washington via an inland passage witnessed by more than 5000 people along the way.[4] The passage included going up the Potomac River and berthing the submarine at the Washington Navy Yard during Christmastime.

Still, a positive decision for the purchase of the submarine was not at hand. On 21 and 24 January 1900, the *New York Times* reported in headlines "Rejection of the Holland Boat", and "Reports on the Holland Boat; Majority of the Navy Board Does Not Favor a Purchase." The negatives regarding the purchase of *Holland VI* primarily stemmed from the Navy's previous government expenditures of the order of $90,000 for the unusable *Plunger.*

In March, after a winter of reconditioning and an almost daily showing of *Holland VI* to various interested personages, an official test course was established on the Potomac River. The one-mile course ran from Fort Washington in Maryland to Mount Vernon in Virginia.

On March 14, the day of the major exhibition, a naval tug with press on board towed the submarine to the test site. Two other vessels provided viewing platforms for naval officials including Admiral Dewey, the Assistant Secretary of the Navy, House and Senate personnel. Among the crew of Holland VI was Admiral Dewey's personal assistant, Lieutenant H. H. Caldwell, who later became the first

---

[4] Jeffrey L. Rodegen, Serving the Silent Service: The Legend of Electric Boat, Write Stuff Syndicate, Inc., 1994, p. 31.

commanding officer of a United States submarine. The submarine demonstrated its obligatory submerging, surfacing, and torpedo firing. Spectators and press alike were duly impressed. There were four more days of successful demonstrations during the next several weeks.

On April 11, 1900, the Navy purchased *Holland VI* for $150,000; and it was turned over to the Navy on April 30. The Navy Torpedo Station at Newport, Rhode Island, was designated as homeport and an all-Navy crew was trained by September with the commissioning the following month.

The new submarine was modestly armed with one forward torpedo tube, three Whitehead torpedoes, and a bow-mount pneumatic dynamite gun. *Holland VI* was small but was considered the most advanced submarine in the world.

Epilogue

A few months later in September 1900, the newly-acquired and only United States submarine participated in naval war games in the Atlantic off Newport, Rhode Island, as part of the defending fleet. During the exercises, Caldwell as Commanding Officer of the *Holland* made the impressive maneuver of bringing the submarine within hailing distance of the hostile flagship *Kearsarge*. Caldwell announced to the battleship, "Hello *Kearsarge*, you are blown to atoms. This is the *Holland*."[5] Caldwell's action may have been premature, but it was certainly prescient.

The United States now had one submarine and the related technology would gradually grow and improve. Until World War I, 14 years away, acceptance of the submarine would come grudgingly from many quarters (including the

---

[5] John Niven et al,. Dynamic America, General Dynamics with Doubleday, n.d., p. 69.

Navy), but submarines would be built. It is noteworthy that even after the lessons of World War I and its obvious offensive capability, the submarine in 1919 would be discounted in favor of capital ships as the ultimate naval weapon. [6]

Between 1900 and 1916, the Electric Boat company built 49 submarines with the Holland design and patents for the United States Navy. Holland, with his primary patents belonging to the Electric Boat Company and a continuing downgrading of his role, resigned at the end of 1904. Lacking his patents, the navy in 1907 disavowed Holland's recent submarine designs. The later years were marked by litigation with his financial backers. One of his last inventions was an apparatus to enable sailors to escape from a damaged submarine. Aircraft and problems of flight were the focus of his creative energies until his death in 1914 at the brink of World War I.

A tribute to Holland occurred a half-century later. The United States Navy built an experimental test-bed diesel submarine, *Albacore* (AGSS 569), commissioned in 1953 and reconfigured five times (1953 through 1971). In one of the phases, "the control surfaces were moved forward of the propeller, a position which Holland had used in the initial configuration of *Holland VI* and had changed, under pressure...Holland had the right idea after all."[7]

Commissioned in 1959, the nuclear-powered fish-shaped *Skipjack* (SSN 585), which at the time was considered the fastest submarine in the world, reflected Holland's original naval architectural concepts to give submarines enhanced underwater performance.

---

[6] Kenneth J. Hagan, This People's Navy: The Making of American Sea Power, The Free Press, New York, 1991, p. 296.
[7] Brayton Harris, Submarines: A Political, Social, and Military History, Berkley Books, New York, 1997, p. 356.

The Electric Boat Company, just prior to the sale of the *Holland VI*, had expressions of interest in building submarines from countries such as Turkey, Venezuela, Mexico, Sweden, Norway, Denmark, and Russia. In the fall of 1900, the Electric Boat Company made licensing arrangements for the construction of Holland submarines with Vickers Sons and Maxim Limited as the builders in Great Britain. Thus, the British submarine fleet became a reality with the Holland patents.

The *Congressional Record* of 4 December 1902 included the J. P. Holland Torpedo Boat Company and the Electric Boat Company as part of the Military Industrial Complex. Submarine building, although small in the Navy's budget, was in the national and international limelight.

In 1904, after the recent addition of five Holland-type submarines to its Navy built at the insistence of British Admiral Sir John Fisher, First Sea Lord and creator of Britain's dreadnought fleet, he made a most sagacious comment relative to submarines when he said, "In all seriousness, I don't think it is even faintly realized—the immense impending revolution which the submarine will effect as offensive weapons of war."[8] Ten years later, in 1914, Lord Fisher wrote in a still more positive vein that the submarine "is the coming type of war vessel for sea fighting."[9]

The August 25, 1905 *New York Times* headlined on page 1 "President Takes Plunge in Submarines: Remains Below the Surface for Fifty-five Minutes, He Maneuvers the Vessel Himself..." On the same day on the editorial page under "Our Submerged President," Theodore Roosevelt was

[8] Philip K. Lundeberg, "Undersea Warfare and Allied Strategy in World War I, Part I: to 1919." Smithsonian Journal of History, 1996, p. 4.
[9] James Phinney Baxter 3rd, Scientists Against Time, 1946, reprinted. M.I.T. Press, Cambridge, MA, 1968, p. x.

cautioned to restrain himself from doing those *stunts* of adventure.

Accounts of Roosevelt's adventure indicate that the weather and the sea state on that day were far from ideal. The President's role during the trial trip was not as passenger but as participant with crew of seven. At one point in the submarine's practice dives in Long Island Sound, the President operated the controls. The submarine was *Plunger*, the Navy's second submarine, commissioned in 1903 and except for an additional 20 feet in length identical with *Holland VI*. Following his trip on board *Plunger*, the President issued a directive that enlisted men detailed to submarines be granted an additional $10 per month as hazardous duty pay.[10] Under his Presidency, the Navy grew in numbers of ships while naval personnel increased from 25,050 in 1901 to 44,500 at the end of 1909.

In spite of obvious shortcomings, the submarine had arrived. By the eve of World War I in 1914, there were 400 submarines in 16 navies. They were not all Holland deigns, but his impact was seminal.

---

[10] Nathan Miller, Theodore Roosevelt: a Life, Morrow, New York, 1992, p. 41.

CONVOY: THE FORGOTTEN YEARS
1919-1939

Part One

Earlier Convoys

Convoying merchant ships at sea to protect them from marauders has been an almost intuitive naval tactic possibly since the Phoenicians. In 1673, Samuel Pepys, then Secretary of the Admiralty Office, instituted a convoy system to protect British trade from damage by Dutch privateers. Convoying was certainly successfully achieved during the age of fighting sail in the 16th, 17th, and 18th Centuries against the surface raiders called cruisers. The British convoy acts of 1793 and 1798 declared it illegal for Britain's overseas commerce to proceed unescorted in wartime in the age of sail. There was a three-hundred-year custom of convoys in Holland, France and Great Britain.

Regarding Convoy

Examination of acoustic detection of enemy submarines during both World War I and II brings one's attention to convoying merchant ships. With a long and successful historical record of navies directly protecting merchant ships, it might be assumed that this tactic would be quickly invoked in a 20th century war. Yet during the first several years of World War I, there were English military and civilian leaders and other members of the Allies who, in the face of available evidence favorable to convoying merchant ships, dissented regarding the need and the advantages to be gained by its implementation. Although begrudgingly, merchant ship convoying was implemented by the Allies May 1917 and was hugely successful for the remainder of the war.

After the armistice, November 1918, following the quick success of convoying during the last one and one-half years of World War I, the tactic and consideration of its planning or readiness seem to have been put aside or forgotten. Further, naval historian S. W. Roskill, RN noted "...not one exercise in the protection of a slow moving mercantile convoy against submarines took place between 1919 and 1939." The negative attitude toward merchant ship protection at the beginning of World War II still persisted in some quarters.

Submarine Century Begins

A century of submarines began in April 1900 when the newly-formed Electric Boat Company and one of its subsidiaries, the John P. Holland Torpedo Boat Company, sold the submarine *Holland VI* to the United States Navy. This was a landmark event, establishing the submarine on the international scene. The successful submarine and Holland's patents for their construction provided the basis for an extraordinary interest in submarines and submarine building by most of the world's leading countries. By the eve of World War I fourteen years later, there were 400 submarines in sixteen navies armed with torpedoes, deck guns and mines.

By 1900, worldwide naval thinking was strongly influenced by the writings of Alfred Thayer Mahan, an Annapolis graduate, longtime career officer, and teacher at the U.S. Naval War College, whose books on naval strategy were accepted by the naval elite in all the maritime powers.

Mahan's teachings were focused on single, decisive, offensive naval engagements with enemy battle ships. The concept of a clash of the modern armadas came in part from his widely read and accepted conclusions in The Influence of Sea Power upon History: 1660-1783 (1890) and The Influence of Sea Power upon the French Revolution and Empire, 1793-1812 (1892). The unprecedented technological changes in ships and armament made the scene in World War I vastly different from the world of sail so well understood by Mahan. Acceptance of the submarine as more than a coastal defense craft and an appreciation of its potential as an offensive naval craft would require new generations of naval officers in the post-Mahan era.

On April 20, 1904, Admiral Sir John Fisher, First Sea Lord and creator of Britain's dreadnought fleet, made a most prescient comment relative to submarines when he said, "In all seriousness, I don't think it is even faintly realized...the immense impending revolution which the submarine will effect as offensive weapons of war."

The same year, extensive at-sea exercises were held off Portsmouth, England, in Spithead Strait. Six recently, completed British submarines of the Holland design, now equipped with a periscope, were part of the operation. It quickly became apparent that capital ships involved would require extensive destroyer screening to protect them from the submarines. Alarm over the submarine's effectiveness was heightened by the fact that there was no method for detecting a submerged submarine (even though when totally submerged they were vulnerable to mines). No further consideration was given to antisubmarine defense until the War. The submarines fared well in the exercise.

Later, on the brink of World War I in 1913, Fisher wrote a memorandum, "The Submarine and Commerce," and noted "...if the submarine is used at all against commerce, she must sink her capture." Among the higher echelons including Winston Churchill, then First Lord of the Admiralty, First Sea Lord Prince Louis Battenberg, and Commodore of Submarines Roger Keyes, there was opposition and lack of acceptance of Fisher's view about submarines sinking their foes. Fisher was somewhat alone in his views at the time, but the early conduct of the U-boat commanders in the opening months of World War I supported Fisher's observation.

A well-turned comment regarding submarines at this time appeared in a history of oceanography written by Susan Schlee. At the onset of World War I, the United States, France, and Britain seemed to have taken the advice offered a Prime Minister by a First Lord of the Admiralty in 1804, on the occasion of seeing Robert Fulton's plans for a submarine: "Don't look at it, and don't touch it. If we take it up other nations will, and it will be the greatest blow at our supremacy on the sea that can be imagined."[1]

In spite of historical evidence favorable to convoying, the Allies in World War I waited nearly three years until April 1917 to invoke convoy as a way to effectively curb the very successful U-boat sinking of merchant ships. Earlier in February, there were 150 U-boats involved in unrestricted warfare. The effect of German submarines sinking one of every four merchant ships leaving England was catastrophic. In addition to the extreme death toll, the loss of many ships and their cargoes produced a number of severe shortages. By April, England's heavily-imported food supply was down to sixty days and in June, oil essential to both military and industrial needs was down to a three-month supply. During the twenty-one years between the two World Wars, the submarine improved in every respect along with its weapons and in numbers. Fully-adequate resources for broad implementation of merchant

---

[1] S. Schlee, The Edge of an Unfamiliar World: A History of Oceanography, Dutton, New York, 1973, p. 245.

ship convoying were not immediately available in Great Britain at the start of World War II. Although full United States participation in the new war was delayed for more than two years, ample resources for merchant ship convoying would be in short supply until 1943.

Slowness to respond to the U-boat havoc at the start of World War I may possibly be laid to the low regard in which the gradually-developing and-evolving submarine was held. An item in print in 1902 referred to the submarine as not an honest weapon. Other comments were also demeaning. The underwater craft, small and lacking even some of the elementary needs for adequate crew habitability, was held in derision by some. To others, the submarine was identified with coast defense and the recourse of a nation with a second-rate navy. Navy culture envisioned itself as an aggressive force, not a defensive one; the submarines were not viewed as vital in the offensive concept yet by some, the submarine was seen as a craft that could undermine navies.

In *Some Principles of Maritime Strategy* (1911), Sir Julian S. Corbett observed that commerce raiding was not likely to be strategically decisive so convoys would be unnecessary. He appreciated the role that submarines would play against capital ships. However, he did not grasp the extent to which submarines would become the cruisers of the future.

Flawed perception of the then narrowly-practical submarine a little more than a decade on the international naval scene revealed its strongest feature when German U-boats adopted the *guerre de course* approach to offensive action. This found the Allies totally surprised and unprepared with regard to countering the U-boat's success. In 1915, when Germany was the first to launch unrestricted submarine warfare, even those naval officers versed in submarine warfare as it was understood at the time were disconcerted.

Previously, it was understood that submarine warfare would be restrained by maritime law and the unacceptable ethics involved in submarine sinkings. In some instances, either using gunfire or placing an explosive charge would finish off the merchant ship under attack by an enemy submarine. This provided an assured sinking. International law at the start of the war required verification of cargo by an enemy submarine prior to combat engagement. Litigation regarding some World War I U-boat sinkings of merchant ships continued into the 1920s.

U-boat accomplishments and the beginnings of antisubmarine warfare (ASW) were concurrent. The concept of submarine against submarine had its origin in the search for ways to counter the U-boats in the desperate times of World War I. The remainder of the 20th Century witnessed the unending development of ASW--always off balance as submarines gained acceptance and were provided with improved operational abilities and better weapons. A further obstacle to success against enemy submarines is the ocean, the submarine's operating medium. It is not transparent.

World War I

England--German Submarines--Convoy

Within six weeks of England's declaration of war against Germany August 4, 1914, Germany's U-boats torpedoed four English cruisers with a loss of more than 1600 lives. By the end of 1914, U-boats successfully moved on merchant ships and asserted rights as their own referees at the scene of the encounter. In addition to the sinkings of merchant ships, the number of ships damaged became excessive and created additional burdens on the already overworked British shipyards. Germany began its first unrestricted U-boat warfare between February and April 1915. Before the first year of the war was over U-boat sinkings outweighed ship losses to any other weapon. The true nature of submarine warfare was emerging. Tactics and

69

weapons for antisubmarine warfare were not immediately at hand.

Convoying military troopships was invoked immediately. Two weeks after the start of the war, the British Expeditionary Force, including men, equipment and stores safely negotiated the crossing to France with the aid of convoying. Hundreds of thousands of Allied troops were successfully transported using convoys between India, Egypt, England, and France. In October, a Canadian contingent of soldiers and equipment in a convoy of more than thirty ships transited unharmed to England. Convoys had not been forgotten. Merchant ships with civilian passengers, crews, and cargoes were not in the purview of the Admiralty's consideration as candidates for the advantages of convoy. There were occasional exceptions to this approach to convoying.

Arguments against merchant ship convoying focused on several concepts which were ultimately proved not correct. The large number of merchant ships now needing protection was an additional consideration. In earlier times when convoy had been invoked, the number of merchant ships was considerably smaller. There was misunderstanding regarding the number of escort ships required per convoy. Later, the ratio of escorts per merchant ships proved to be a much smaller number than that originally thought by the Admiralty. The skills of the merchant marine ship captains and crews to participate in convoying were also underrated during these early deliberations. Delays in shipping due to organizing convoys were an additional point of argument.

The tools available for countering the U-boats in the beginning of the war were limited. Visual U-boat sighting was the chief method and confined to daylight. Mines and gunfire were the weapons. Sweeping vast areas of the ocean visually with limited numbers of search vessels to locate a single 200-foot long U-boat, which might or might not be located on the surface, was typical. Earlier, Mahan succinctly addressed the issue by claiming "the results of the convoy system warrants the inference that, when properly systematized and applied, it will have more success than hunting for individual marauders—a process which, even when most thoroughly planned, still resembles looking for a needle in a haystack." Proponents of this Mahanian view were scarce.

As the war progressed, improved mines, depth charges, and the beginnings of elementary acoustic underwater detection equipment appeared toward the end of the conflict. Radio communications for the searchers were still in a basic stage of development. Blimps, planes, and submarines were used in convoy and antisubmarine efforts before the war ended.

Convoy Deadlock

The British Navy, even with the accumulated evidence of U-boat prowess in the fall of 1916, was reluctant to invoke convoy for merchant shipping. The advantages and potential of the concept of convoy and its subtle ramifications were not understood. The Admiralty's dilemma in dealing with the U-boat problem and general acceptance of the submarine as a part of modern navies may be viewed by considering the following: the submarine was still a relatively new development and its stealth properties made it unique, the U-boat success as a commerce raider was not expected; and further, as mentioned previously, equipment for combating submarines was not at hand. It was an unconventional weapon intruding on a centuries-old conventional navy. Similar attitudes towards the submarine were held in the United States Navy.

Even in the face of the sinkings the preceding year January 1917 found the Admiralty publishing an official view declining convoy as a requirement for safe passage.

John Winton wrote in *CONVOY: The Defence of Sea Trade 1890-1990*, (1983) "the pamphlet which stated, quite definitely and emphatically, that convoy was not a sound method of defending trade." Another severe blow to the already jeopardized merchant vessels came in the German announcement 31 January that unrestricted submarine warfare would begin the next day. With forty-six U-boats at sea, extreme losses would occur in the following six months.

This crisis could no longer be ignored. Commitment of scarce resources for convoy escort did not occur until after several more months of negotiation, haggling, and with encouragement from the United States. Rear Admiral William S. Sims, USN, assigned to London to cooperate and keep the United States Navy Department apprised of the British scene, arrived on 9 April 1917. Sims' secret departure for England was just prior to America's entry into the War. Secretary of the Navy Josephus Daniels, briefed Sims regarding the Wilson Administration's views on the British Navy's performance in the War. Two points were that the British had not been vigorous enough in their efforts to curb the U-boat destruction of shipping and that all ships ought to be convoyed. The convoy dilemma heightened when on the night of April 17 thirty-four ships were sunk.

Shortly after his arrival three days after the American declaration of war, Sims promptly encouraged a study to be undertaken regarding the practical aspects of convoying. The study was quickly completed and acknowledged the practicability of convoying. Sims, a senior and experienced officer, by his maturing pro-convoy stance helped to expedite the resolution by the Admiralty to undertake convoy to counter the U-boats' decimation of the merchant shipping. His position stated "...It therefore seems to go without question that the only course of action for use to pursue is to revert to the ancient practice of convoy. This can be purely an offensive action, because if we concentrate our shipping into convoy and protect it with our naval forces we will thereby force the enemy to carry out his mission, to encounter naval forces...we will have adopted the essential principle of concentration." An enhanced program of merchant ship convoying was undertaken within the month.

David Lloyd George, with only a few weeks in office as Prime Minister, was finally able to prod the reluctant Admiralty to adopt convoying as a last resort to stem the huge merchant ship losses to U-boats. The end of April saw the initial steps by the Admiralty to convoy all vessels (except those above fifteen knots), British, Allied, and neutral. An April 30 convoy from Gibraltar to the British Isles was a success. Transatlantic convoys would be next. Requests for U.S. Navy escort participation were initially greeted with the same reluctance and arguments that the Admiralty had been using. A particular point was the ratio of escorts to the number of merchant ships, but eventually this was no longer an issue.

The destroyer with its high speed and torpedoes proved to be the convoy escort's cornerstone. Sloops, trawlers, old cruisers and old battleships were included in the merchant ship escorts. It was quickly learned that convoys of as many as twenty or thirty merchant ships could be successfully managed. Equipping convoyed merchant ships with arms enhanced safe transits. In the three-month period of May through July 1917, the total losses in convoy and independent losses through U-boat attack in the Atlantic and British home waters after the introduction of convoy were 383 ships sunk. Of 8707 ships convoyed, 27 were lost. Independent losses comprised the remainder.

By the following year, 1918, the shipping loss fell by two-thirds. Antisubmarine warfare (ASW) involving Allied resources from Britain, Italy, U.S., and Japan included 400 surface vessels, 216 seaplanes. 85 large flying boats, and 75 blimps. On a manpower basis, it has been estimated that 100 men from the Allies were needed for each German on a submarine.   Another evaluation concluded that 25 Allied warships and 100 aircraft per U-boat were needed.

The submarine changed the way war at sea was conducted. Enemy submarines complicated the means and character of naval warfare in different ways. The demand for naval resources to prosecute ASW and convoy escort obligations was extreme. Sometimes this led to force dispersion. Convoying was successful in saving ships and lives. In addition to the vast amount of resources, manpower, and platforms, additional time was required to organize the convoys. The speed of transit was slower to accommodate the merchant ships. Calculations indicated a 25 percent loss in carrying capability when convoy is in use. By the end of the War in late 1918, England had between 400 and 500 destroyers in commission to meet the critical needs for convoys and patrols. The U-boats did not control the seas, they denied access. Safe passage came at a price.

As the war ended, ASW patrolling and convoying were being brought to bear. The resources included ships, submarines, airplanes, and blimps. The weapons were mines, depth charges, steel nets, and torpedoes. By 1918, acoustic detection of submarines was in the embryo stage and slowly evolving. Also, it would seem that U-boats and the success of *guerre de course* would have been indelibly imprinted on future naval thinking and planning. Convoying prevented the Allies from losing the war in 1917. The leading maritime nations of the world would give their attention at varying levels to ASW for the remainder of the century.

As World War II began, the repeated success of the U-boats and availability of the means to counter them was again limited. The reasons for this are not totally clear. Preparedness, support and awareness of convoying merchant shipping were lacking. United States implementation of the convoy tactic in the latter part of the War for merchant ship protection from the again-successful U-boats in 1941-42 was not swift. Consideration of the period between the close of World War I and the beginning of World War II may provide some insight.

CONVOY; THE FORGOTTEN YEARS
1919-1939

Part Two

By the end of the First World War, using accumulated convoy data from various sources and applying statistical methods, British navy analysts easily affirmed the efficacy of the convoy tactic in a modern naval war. Lessons learned during the war also included the tactic of submarine versus submarine, which would evolve gradually in the years ahead.

Merchant ship protection from the U-boat was provided during World War I primarily by patrolling the seas (guarding the sea lanes) and convoy escorting. Patrolling to counter enemy submarines steadfastly held its place as the primary U-boat countermeasure in the minds of some senior navy personnel in the years after World War I. In spite of convoying's documented successes, the reason for that bias toward patrolling perhaps was because it could be viewed as an *offensive* Navy posture and more in keeping with Navy aims.

The convoy concept made the enemy submarine confront defended merchant ships rather than independent ships defenseless against the U-boat. Patrolling expended scarce resources searching for enemy submarines in large ocean areas and in unknown locations without adequate tools for detection and localization of the U-boat, whether submerged or surfaced by day or night.

Convoying was a positive approach to resolving U-boat interdiction of merchant ships; it brought the enemy to a defended target. In the interim years, the subtle aspects of convoy were not always easily grasped by the military and elected officials. The effectiveness of convoying was available in the records.

The victorious countries involved in the war were determined to keep the hard-earned peace. A series of international peace conferences and treaties were held during the period 1921 to 1936. Reduction of capital ships was a main consideration. At the same time, submarines and their weapons steadily improved. In several countries, research was undertaken to better the methods for detection of submarines. Progress in this area would benefit both patrolling and convoying in the event of a future naval war.

Without the urgency of a wartime environment, planning and preparing for Navy convoying of merchant ships in time of war did not present itself as a critical issue nor one generally of much interest during the 20 years of peace. The nonconformist aspects of submarines and their use compared to surface craft came to national and international attention primarily in arguments concerning the abolition of submarines or restraining submarine actions towards merchant shipping during wartime. Full acceptance of submarines as an integral part of the panoply of naval weapons was not held in all quarters of the world's navies in spite of their increasing number.

In several countries some of the antisubmarine warfare ongoing research focused on the development and implementation of acoustic detection of submarines. If successful, this was seen by some as a means to remove the convoying requirement.

The ambivalence of certain naval professionals regarding submarines in this period while the submarine and its weapons were developing tended to obscure convoying and the acquisition of the necessary resources for successful implementation in the event of war. A measure of the necessary anti-submarine resources to help defeat the U-boat and sink 200 U-boats in World War I has been estimated to include 5000 ships, hundreds of miles of steel nets, and a million depth charges, mines, bombs, and shells.[1]

National and International Naval Concerns 1919-1939

Disarmament was of considerable importance starting with the early post-War years. War was unthinkable during the decade after the War and beyond. The enormous debts of the vanquished and the victors alike and the excessive loss of lives and casualties were strongly perceived and remembered. There were multiple reasons for disarmament, some of safeguarding peace, and some driven by economic considerations, which worsened during the 1920s.

A view as to how the submarine was held in the minds of some is expressed in a paper given in March 1919 at a British War Cabinet meeting held to discuss future warfare research. Lord Weir, Secretary of the State for the Air Force, asked "What would the House of Commons say to the creation of a new big institution for research in connection with warfare at a time when we may be presumed to be establishing peace conditions on a stable footing? If for instance, the submarine were definitely ruled out of warfare, would not the strongest argument in favor of the Admiralty scheme disappear?"[2]

---

[1] Len Deighton, <u>Blood, Tears, and Folly: An Objective Look at World War II</u>, Harper Collins, NY, 1993, p. 16.
[2] Willem, Hackmann, <u>Seek and Strike</u>, Her Majesty's Printing Office, London, 1954, p. 99-100.

Starting in 1920, the Ten Year Rule prevailed in Britain. The rule implied that the British Empire would not be engaged in any great war during the next ten years. It provided a reason for reducing military expenditures and continued several years beyond 1930. All the armed forces were impacted by reductions in support.

Views regarding the submarine by naval and government figures during the decades between the world wars were diverse with generally no consensus among the five powers: France, United States, Great Britain, Italy, and Japan. A comment regarding submarines was made at this time "…that such methods as the Germans used will never be employed again, but need not be feared that any civilized nation would adopt them…"[3]

Moreover, as early as 1922, with Germany banned from making submarines and other military weapons by the Versailles Treaty, German civilians were designing new German submarines for a Dutch firm, a front for certain German shipyards, located in The Hague. Later, experimental models were constructed in Holland and Spain.

Britain's hesitant position regarding submarines in the postwar period was frequently voiced as favoring the abolition of the submarine as a weapon of war. This view was taken at the Versailles Peace Conference, in the 1921-22 Washington Peace Conference, in 1925, and at the London Conference in 1930 and the last London Conference in 1936. Beyond abolition of the submarine, a position aimed at reducing the international submarine tonnage or restricting submarine activities was taken, mostly without great success.

In 1927, the British Director of Naval Intelligence focused on a possible reason for this anti-submarine position

---

[3] Ironclad to Trident: 100 Years of Defence Commentary, Brassey's, 1888-1986, p. 111.

by Great Britain "...trying to influence other governments against submarines because Britain herself has 'more to fear from submarines than has any other power'..."[4]

Article 22 of the London Naval Treaty of 1930 agreed to by the United States and Great Britain approached the submarine problem by stating that in time of war "...a warship, whether surface vessel or submarine, may not sink or render incapable of navigation a merchant vessel without first having placed passengers, crew and ship's papers in a place of safety..." A further consideration provided that the merchant ships would not be armed during peacetime. Later, the Third Reich officially agreed to this article on 23 November 1936.

Hitler's coming to power in 1934 was immediately followed with his flaunting of the Versailles Treaty by Germany ordering 24 of the previously-mentioned Finnish model submarines and two of the Spanish version.

A body of naval opinion preserved the anti-convoy viewpoint throughout the 1930s. A March 1935 House of Commons speech by Lord Stanley of the Admiralty reflects such. Stanley assured the house that the convoy system would not be introduced at once on the outbreak of war. All the pre-April 1917 arguments against the need to have merchant ship convoying were recycled 18 years later in 1935.

The Anglo-German naval agreement was reached on June 18, 1935. Germany was once again legally permitted to build and operate a fleet of submarines. The next month Winston Churchill observed that the German Navy was meager. Other comments included "today Germany has no submarines." Germany launched the first U-boat four months later. The following year the London Submarine Protocol, 3

---

[4] Hackmann, op cit, p. 126.

September, cited that Germany would adhere strictly to the international prize law, which provided for safety of merchant ship passengers and crews in time of war.

During the 1920s and 30s, submarines and airplanes continued to be regarded as fleet reconnaissance and attack elements. However, naval strategist French Admiral Raoul Castex envisioned renewal of the use of submarines as commerce raiders.

The late 1930s found increasing numbers of sophisticated submarines with improved weapons on the international scene. The submarine's record as a successful merchant ship raider was available from the preceding war. It would seem that this would lead to positive national positions regarding convoying merchant ships and with it appropriate planning and preparation in the event of war.

Planning for the convoying merchant ships finally received some attention in Britain in 1937. The Air Staff and the Admiralty after further arguments agreed that convoying should be adopted in the event of war but only if the enemy resumed unrestricted submarine warfare. This allowed the admiralty to create a worldwide shipping control organization, and by 1939 the planning was well advanced.

Acoustic Detection of Submarines

Modest improvements in the acoustic detection of submarines were made on both sides of the Atlantic by November 1918. In England and the United States leading scientists and engineers, including Nobel award winners, turned their attention to solving the problem of submarine detection. By the end of World War I, submerged submarines could be located. Some of the unresolved equipment limitations included enemy submarine depth determination, detecting in rough seas, and range. Also, the vagaries of acoustic propagation in seawater were yet to be determined.

After the war ended, England continued investigating acoustic detection at a secret level. Similar work was undertaken in the United States. Because the detection equipment was classified, sharing of information did not occur prior to 1939. Equipment testing with submarines under realistic conditions was not substantial.[5] The British acoustic detection equipment was known as Asdic (an acronym). It was advanced compared to the World War I equipment but limited in its capabilities. Civilian and naval observers of the equipment tended to become over-optimistic. Some erroneously concluded that enemy submarines would not be a problem in the event of wars because of availability of the equipment.

Some comments made by Winston Churchill in *Gathering Storm* about Asdic are illuminating. On June 15, 1938, Churchill was on board a destroyer for an Asdic demonstration with Royal Navy submarines as targets. In 1948, Churchill noted that in 1938 he and others overrated the capability of the underwater acoustics detection of enemy submarines. The performance limitations of the early systems were not fully grasped by the fall of 1939. The optimism regarding the expected performance of Asdic led to lack of preparation to make up for the equipment limitations which became apparent.

Advancement of military technology in the United States during the long peacetime period was slow, due heavily to lack of fiscal support for research and development. The funds available for military technology development were a small percentage of the overall military

---

[5] "Always demonstrated in perfect weather by well rehearsed crews, it enabled a confident Admiralty to declare the U-boat to be a weapon of the past." Deighton, op. cit., p. 21.

expenditure. Research project security classification and the independence of the various branches of the armed forces were additional barriers to progress. Academic and private sector scientific and engineering personnel did not have broad participation with the current government military research laboratories. The Naval Research Laboratory opened in Washington in 1923, and in conjunction with several industrial activities became the center for the development of enemy submarine detection equipment. By 1933, fifteen destroyers and five submarines were equipped with echo ranging acoustic detection equipment. At the end of the decade, additional progress was made regarding the numbers of installations and the beginnings of adequate training for equipment operators and use were initiated.

Closing Comment

Navy problems and priorities during the years between the wars placed merchant ship convoying in an obscure role. Mahanian thinking with the capital ship at its focus still prevailed. Aircraft and aircraft carriers began to be acknowledged, and some inroads in naval thinking and planning were made in these areas during these years.

Decreased naval budgets and the high costs and years of construction time for the large ships placed construction of smaller ships for convoy escorting in a low priority position. The shorter time requirement for the building of convoy escort ships may have accounted for their low priority.

The high performance expectations of the 1930s submarine detection equipment as cited above led to a downplaying of the enemy submarine's capabilities. In retrospect, even if the performance was as anticipated, there were only limited numbers of vessels. equipped with the detection equipment; as a further problem, the number of skilled operators was insufficient.

As late as November 1938, a retired German vice admiral noted in an article "nothing substantial has as yet been done in England (and equally in France) for the protection of oceanic convoys." Soviet Admiral Gorshkov observed in 1976 that the "American navy came into War (II) totally unprepared to protect merchant vessels from submarine strikes."[6]

Even though analysis of convoy performance presented evidence that convoying did not cause excessive delays in shipping and did save lives and ships, there were those in the Admiralty and in public office in 1939, twenty years later at the start of World War II, who were overtly not pro-convoy. As late as early 1942, some U. S. Navy personnel were initially not enthusiasts for convoying. A quotation in Morison indicated "when the U-boat hit our coast in January 1942, we were caught with our pants down through lack of anti-submarine vessels" [7]

[6] S. G. Gorshkov, *The Sea Power of the State*, MIT 1976/79, p. 266
[7] S. E. Morison, *The Battle of the Atlantic: September 1939-May 1943*, Little, Brown and Company, Boston, 1988, p. 254.

SLIDE RULE STRATEGY BEGINS

World War II Operations Research

In the fall of 1939, England was again fighting Germany, the same enemy as in World War I. However, advances in the tools of war during the twenty years of peace set the scene far distant from August 1914. The short distance from mainland Europe to England presented a minimal challenge by that time for a military aircraft.

Similarly, scarcity of appropriate antisubmarine weapons, resources and tactics provided further new formidable tasks in hunting an improved enemy submarine, always a complex target operating in an opaque environment. U-boats of 1939 were faster underwater, could operate at greater depths, and maneuver more skillfully. They were quieter, with longer endurance and tougher hulls.

The severity of the U-boat problem led Vannevar Bush, President Roosevelt's adviser and chief contact on all matters of military technology including the atomic bomb, to observe in his memoir Pieces of the Action, "The United States came very close too close---to being defeated in each war by the submarine."[1] After the war, Winston Churchill wrote, "The only thing that ever really frightened me during

---

[1] Vannevar Bush, *Pieces of the Action*, William Morrow and Company, Inc., New York, NY, 1970,   p. 70.

the war was the U-boat peril."[2] Statistics on U-boat sinkings support the post-war reflections of Bush and Churchill.

U-Boat Sinkings

September 1939-April 1943 (44 months) **193**

May-June-July 1943 **100**

Credit for this remarkable shift in the antisubmarine war against the U-boats stems from a number of activities, efforts, and approaches by many individuals. Success was not instantaneous. The progress beginning in May 1943 was hard earned. The introduction and evolution of operations research, the application of mathematics and the scientific method to military operations, was one of many contributions leading to the defeat of the U-boat.

World War I was fought with weapons available at its start. World War II, sometimes referred to as the physicists' and engineers' war, witnessed a continuing stream of new weapons, frequently complex, and raising difficult operational questions on occasion beyond the purview of the military.

England's late-1930s introduction of radar in conjunction with air defense epitomizes WW II high technology. New, untried, extremely complicated, costly and needed, it was highly effective when properly used. The military user required assistance from the scientists who conceived it and the engineers who manufactured it.

---

[2] Winston S. Churchill, *The Second World War*, Vol. II. p. 598.

Operations research was not prescribed. It evolved, as participation by civilian physicists, engineers, mathematicians, astronomers, physiologists applied their scientific methods to equipment performance with the field military operators on land, air and shipboard. Optimizing system performance and solving problems based on careful analysis of data collected from direct experience in real time operations in a wartime environment followed scientific methods bring the term **slide rule strategy** into use. Operations research improvements by factors of 3 or 10 were common. This level of contribution was out of proportion to the amount of effort spent. By 1942, acceptance of the methodology brought formal operations research groups to all three of Britain's military services.

Operations research techniques used by civilian scientists contributed to a first defeat for Hitler, with the UK winning the Battle of Britain (air warfare) in the summer of 1940. Increased mastery in sinking U-boats starting in May 1943 is attributed likewise in part to operations research. Because of this and other successful WW II applications of the method, today every branch of the military has its own operations research group involving both military and civilian personnel. Military operations research provided the logistic planning for Operation Desert Storm. The United States National Security Agency has its own Center for Operations Research.

Early Operations Research

During the 1800s, two inventors, one a mathematician and other an engineer, contributed significantly to the formulation, expansion and acceptance of operations research as a tool in the 20th Century.

The mathematician and inventor Charles Babbage (1792-1871) contributed to the early formulation of this new field. His book Economy of Machines and Manufactures

(1832) is said to have initiated the field of study known as operational research. It is notable that during this same period, Babbage developed plans for an analytical engine, the forerunner of the digital computer. His participation in establishing the modern English postal system and developing the first reliable actuarial tables reflects his analytical skills and early operational analysis.

In the United States Frederick W. Taylor (1856-1915), an inventor and engineer known as the father of scientific management, provided additional quantitative methods addressing man-machine problems. Taylor applied scientific principles to mechanisms to make them more efficient, conducting scientific measurement of work and productivity in the work place with the workers and the machines. Taylor's work helped to make Henry Ford's precision automobile production line conveyor belt operation possible. Babbage and Taylor are representative of early contributors to operations research.

World War I Efforts

During World War I, I. F. W. Lanchester, a pioneer in the English motor car industry, made fundamental contributions by mathematically describing the outcome of military actions related to numerical and firepower superiority and concentration of forces. He also foresaw the importance of aeronautical efficiency in future great battles. His equations appear in current literature.

In 1915, Lord Tiverton completed a detailed study of strategic bombing anticipating the 1000 plane bombing raids of WW II. A. V. Hill of the experimental section of the Munitions Invention Department of the British Army studied antiaircraft gunnery and developed tactics and procedures to enhance the effectiveness of antiaircraft fire.

Thomas A. Edison, as a member of the Navy Consulting Board during WW I considering the antisubmarine problem, concluded that sinking German submarines was only one means of saving merchant ships. He directed his efforts to a study of the statistics of enemy submarine activities to evolve strategic plans for optimal merchant ship movements across the Atlantic Ocean. The impact of his findings is not clear. A 1953 paper in Operations Research commented "Nor did Edison's work seem to have had lasting effect on the U. S. Navy, judging by the need to rediscover his procedures at the start of World War II."[3]

Lewis Richardson, a British ambulance driver in World War I who believed mathematical equations could quantify patterns of war, gathered data in his off-duty time. After the War, he compiled his statistical data and developed mathematical equations to predict wartime behavior. In World War II, the British armed forces found extensive use for his equations.

During the twenty years between the wars, while all the tools of war and communications moved forward there was no significant progress in operations research, tactics and countermeasures to combat improved weaponry.

World War II

Great Britain

The development of defense against enemy aircraft had an increasing national priority as early as 1935. Large numbers of capable and creative civilian scientific and technical talent began to be drawn together to address the development of new air defense oriented military equipment. The aim was to use scientific and technical knowledge to strengthen the current methods of defense against hostile

---

[3] *Journal of Operations Research,* Vol. 1. 1953, p. 83.

aircraft. As the war began, the extreme national danger and risk to life and property by the weapons of the new war and the significant initial success of the enemy brought additional personnel to the problems.

By September 1939 and the onset of war, a large part of the anti-aircraft defense system, later known as (early warning) radar, was manned and operating along all of the east and southeast coasts of England. Some of the country's best academic researchers achieved this considerable development. Their scientific methodology involved techniques for analyzing system performance by measurement, collection of data. statistics, analysis and optimization of the man-machine interface relationships.

Battle of Britain July to September 1940

The first major battle fought entirely in the air was the consequence of Germany's mid-July initiative to prepare for an invasion of England by air bombardment. German Luftwaffe outnumbered the British Fighter Command. The British front line defense fighter planes numbered about 600. The Germans, with 1300 bombers and dive-bombers and 900 single-engined and 300 twin-engined fighters, were formidable.

British fighter interceptors of Spitfires (unsurpassed in any other air force) and more squadrons of Hurricane fighters, plus a well planned and executed tactic, helped to make the smaller number of fighters effectively larger. Countering the German flights consisting of up to 1500 planes per day intent on bombing fighter airfields was a most crucial undertaking for a fighter force of 600 planes, with the fate of the country dependent upon its outcome.

Preparation for fighter interception began in late 1936; experiments were conducted for two years at the R.A.F. Fighter Command station at Biggin Hill to address problems in fighter direction and control led by civilian research engineer B. G. Dickins. During the two years before the availability of operational radar, the experiments used simulated radar data and input from the Observer Corps personnel. This planned effort provided a basis for the successful use of the fighters in the summer of 1940.

The radar chain was operational by 1939. In a report by the first radar station at Bawdsey, the term **operational research** originated. With a limited number of fighter planes, the tactic held the planes on the ground until the right moment. Then control directed the plane to a location within visual sighting of the enemy aircraft. Radar range capability at the time was 120 miles out to sea with 50-mile detection of low-flying aircraft. These experiments integrated the radar into the early warning systems, the Observer Corps, and the fighter direction and control.

With increased British plane production, radar, *operations research* methods, and extremely brave fighter pilots, the German plane losses by mid-September 1940 totaled 1700 and the British 900. With limited German plane production and his attention now focusing on Russia, Hitler put aside his plans to invade England.

P.M.S. Blackett

Blackett served in the Royal Navy at sea during World War I, seeing action in the Falkland Island in 1914 and at the battle of Jutland in 1916. Following the war, he studied physics with Nobel Laureate Lord Ernest Rutherford. He came to be widely known for his research related to the Wilson cloud chamber. Later in 1948, unrelated to his war work, Blackett received the Nobel Prize for his work in nuclear physics and cosmic rays.

Starting in mid-January 1935, Blackett served on the Committee for the Scientific Survey of Air Defence. During the five years of the committee's existence, the development and implementation of radar stands out. Commenting on the U-boat crisis in 1941-42 and Blackett's contributions, a paper[4] reported "Prof. P.M.S. Blackett, whose name will go down in the history of operation research as outstanding, came into the picture to see what could be done."

OR and Antiaircraft Gunnery

By August 1940, antiaircraft batteries around London included new gun-laying sets just out of the laboratory. Blackett, appointed science advisor to the headquarters of the Anti-Aircraft Command at Stanmore, addressed the radar implementation problem. Blackett's young scientists included physiologists, an astronomer, and a mathematician, as well as physicists. Problems addressed related to operational use of radar, guns and predictors at the gun sites and headquarters. The overall problem was the blitz bombing of London and other British cities. At this time, Penguin Books published the first book dealing with the development of operations research.

Blackett's team (referred to as Blackett's Circus) perfected a number of operational recommendations. The Circus worked with the Service operational staffs and against very short deadlines. Results included best use of limited radar resources in gun deployment around London, improved data plotting techniques, design of simple plotting machines, and special schools for training personnel in data handling.

Blackett pointed out a notable change in antiaircraft gunnery effectiveness and its relationship to *operational research*. "At the start of the blitz, when control methods were poor, the 'rounds per bird' as we called this number

---

[4] Charles Goodeve, "Operational Research," *Nature* No. 4089, March 13, 1948, p. 377.

was about 20,000.   As methods and instruments improved this gradually fell to some 4,000 the following summer."[5]

By May 1941, German bomber losses over Britain were more than seven percent.   Improvements in the use of antiaircraft gunnery and the introduction of airborne radar contributed to the increased losses.   The overlay of operational research was a strong contributor.   In addition, increased attention to the Balkans and Russia by Germany also led to a diminishing of the overall bombing of Britain.

U-Boat Problem (Britain)

Upon entering the war with Germany in 1939, England's 1936 naval treaty with the Third Reich did not allow merchant ships to be armed.   From the beginning of the war, the U-boat success rate in sinking naval and merchant ships was high.   To counter the U-boats the Royal Navy hunted them with planes, ships and submarines.   The Navy provided merchant convoys with escorts on some sea routes.

Hunting submarines required submarine detection.   In 1935, British expectations of submarine detection performance were flawed.   It was believed in some quarters that the enemy submarine was no longer a menace to national security.   The Asdic surface ship performance in reality was an average range of the order of 1300 yards with the last 200 yards blind.   Nighttime exercises with submarines were rare prewar.   In retrospect, even if the performance was as anticipated, there were only limited numbers of vessels equipped with the detection equipment; as a further problem, the number of skilled operators was insufficient.   Further in 1939 the Royal Navy supply of mines for ASW was minimal.

---

[5] P.M.S. Blackett, "Operational Research Recollections of Problems Studies, 1940-45." Brassey's Annual, The Armed Forces Yearbook 1953, p. 91-92.

Mahanian thinking with the capital ship at its focus still prevailed. Decreased naval budgets and the expense and long lead-time for capital ships did not allow for small ship construction of ASW, and convoy escort ships were not available in numbers as the war began.

As late as November 1938, a retired German Vice-Admiral noted in an article "Nothing substantial has as yet been done in England (and equally in France) for the protection of oceanic convoys."

Blackett and the Anti-U-boat Campaign

In March 1941, Blackett moved from the Anti-Aircraft Command to the Coastal Command to advise on problems arising from the air war against U-boats. The Coastal Command's purview included antisubmarine operations, convoy protection and attacks on enemy shipping primarily in an offensive role. Blackett established his new operations team as part of the Command's senior staff.

In the next several months, Blackett's research revealed the small number of U-boat sinkings by aircraft dropping depth charges. Pursuing this, the OR team carefully studied in detail air attack reports and provided new insight regarding the estimate of the actual depth of the enemy submarine at the instant of attack. This study brought to light the unsuitability of the standard setting of 100 feet for depth charge detonation.

A depth charge dropped by aircraft near the alerted U-boat's submergence point with a lethal radius of 20 feet and a 100-foot explosive depth frequently led to a successful escape by the U-boat. Enemy submarines operating near or close to the surface escaped damage from the deep explosion depth of the charge. Operations research team analysis suggested a detonation of the order of 25 feet. U-boat sinking rate immediately improved. Related problems included

94

aiming, depth charge size, and spacing between depth charges dropped from the aircraft. Collectively the findings and operational measures from these inquiries brought further improvement.

First usage of OR often brings outstanding results. As systems are refined improvement is sometimes less spectacular. By late spring 1943, mastery of the U-boat problem was at hand due to the coming together of a variety of efforts. OR's role was not in creating the weapons but in providing guidance and influence in their judicious use and successfully assessing the enemy's tactics.

Operations Research Countering the U-boat
1941-1943

Recommending an optimum depth for air dropped depth charges
Securing additional Liberator night bombers for convoy cover
Painting bombers sky color to reduce U-boat sighting
Expediting the night use of Leigh Lights on ASW aircraft
Discerning the use of radar listening devices by U-boats
Promoting the use of large convoys (1944 186-ship convoy)
Implementing High Frequency Direction Finding (HF/DF)

U-Boat Problem (United States)

The U-boat crisis was one of the many defense areas Bush faced when President Roosevelt appointed him chairman of the newly-created National Defense Research Committee (NDRC) on 15 June 1940, the day after Paris fell to the Germans. Within a year, Bush recruited six thousand of the country's leading physicists, chemists, engineers and doctors. By the end of the war, they numbered thirty thousand. From within this vast number of scientists the personnel of operations research talent emerged.

The United States U-boat problem was twofold in December 1941. One was how to efficiently hunt and find U-boats; the other how to defend merchant ships from U-boats. The merchant ship problem needed escorts, better depth charges and air cover. Navy convoy escort vessels were in short supply and no central ASW group or unit existed.

As late as early 1942, some U.S. Navy personnel were initially not enthusiasts for convoying merchant ships. A quotation in Morison "when the U-boats hit our coast in January 1942, we were caught with our pants down through lack of anti-submarine vessels"[6] is concise and apt. In February, Britain gave United States 24 trawlers and 10 corvettes. These additional escorts allowed small East Coast convoys during the day and putting into harbor at night. Soviet Admiral Gorshkov observed in 1976 that "the American Navy came into the War totally unprepared to protect merchant vessels from submarine strike."[7]

U.S. Antisubmarine Warfare Operations Research Group (ASWORG)

The U.S. Navy was aware of British success with ASW due in part to their civilian scientists' operations research. After the first few month of the war, it became apparent that the Navy needed ASW data analysis for tactical decisions. The requisite analytical skills including statistics and probability were not in the purview of the military. In March 1942 the Navy requested Bush's NDRC to provide civilian scientific support in the U-boat campaign to the

---

[6] S. E. Morison, *The Battle of the Atlantic: September 1939-May 1943*, Little, Brown and Company, Boston, 1988, p. 254.

[7] S. O. Gorshkov, *The Sea Power of the State*, MIT, 1976/79, p. 256.

Boston ASW unit. The NDRC appointed MIT acoustic research physicist Philip M. Morse, then at the Harvard Underwater Sound Laboratory, to form the group.

Morse directed the U.S. Navy Operations Research Group from 1942 to 1946 starting in Boston, Massachusetts, with a team of seven at the beginning of May 1942. It grew to seventy-three as the war ended. The members were primarily chosen for their general scientific training and included physicists, mathematicians, chemists, biologists, geologists, actuaries (from the six largest US insurance companies), and a champion chess player.

Beginning efforts analyzed the results of U.S. attacks on U-boats by ships and planes and examined the tactics of finding U-boats. U-boat search studies quickly provided fresh guidance to the Navy. The studies revealed potential search rates in square miles per hour of 75 for radar-equipped destroyers, 1000 for meter radar-equipped aircraft, and 3000 for an aircraft with microwave radar.

A previously-established navy Mine Warfare Operations Group from the Navy Ordnance Laboratory concerned with degaussing all U.S. naval vessels to counter German use of magnetic mines became part of ASWORG. Efforts of this team were especially significant in mining related to Truk, invasion of the Marianas, the battle of the Philippine Sea, and mining Japan's Inland Sea using bombers and fatally damaging Japanese shipping in 1944.

OR effort in the Pacific brought to light that Japanese antiaircraft fire was relatively ineffective at 9,000 to 10,000 feet. Tactics were changed, and U.S. aircraft losses significantly reduced.

In October 1942, ASWORG, at the request of NDRC, arranged to assist the U.S. Army Air Force. Early efforts quickly produced an Army Air Force manual on operational use of radar in sea search, study and report on bombsights and photographic coverage of antisubmarine operations.

Review of ASWORG's record reveals a response time from the inception of an action to implementation in the order of one or two months. The Bay of Biscay anti-U-boat offensive, the destruction of the German blockade-runners in the South Atlantic, and the initiation of large convoys in the Atlantic are representative of quick and successful responses.

May 1943: The Turning Point in the Battle of the Atlantic

The meeting of the allied leaders in Casablanca during early 1943 ended with a fresh and firm resolve to counter the U-boats more aggressively. After this, momentum in the ASW battle in the Atlantic increased steadily with a significant increase in U-boat sinkings beginning in May. By the end of the month, Grand Admiral Doenitz removed his U-boats from the North Atlantic to positions west of the Azores and into the Mediterranean

---

May 1943 The Turning Point

January – April **41** U-boats sunk

May **41** U-boats sunk

Why after years of engagement did the tide turn against the U-boats? Men and materials are essential to success in modern wars. Significantly, the rapidly growing availability of allied weapons, aircraft, and naval ships signaled the end of the period of getting ready to fight.

A further crucial change was the 20 May emergence of Admiral Ernest J. King's Tenth Fleet as the consolidated and centralized command of all Atlantic ASW with the broadest possible support to defeat the U-boat challenge.

Earlier in May, King's specifications for the new fleet included a civilian scientist research statistical analysis component headed by Vannevar Bush. ASWORG became part of the Tenth Fleet in August and moved from Boston to Washington, DC. The OR group evolved into a center for the entire U.S. ASW effort. An IBM state-of-the-art data processing system provided help in analyzing and tracking the expanding U-boat data. A large percentage of the OR team eventually widely scattered at various Navy and Army commands in both the Atlantic and Pacific.

Scientists' recommendations on tactics and even strategy were included in the decision processes. As Admiral King pointed out later, "...Operations research, bringing scientists in to analyze the technical import of the fluctuations between measure and counter measure, made it possible to speed up our reaction rate in several critical areas."

Summary

The impact of the civilian operations research scientists, engineers and others with scientific orientation is abundantly clear upon examination of WW II weapons and weapon systems from aspects of research, development, production, introduction and implementation by the military. OR civilian scientists assisted the military in fighting the war both in the continental U.S. and *in situ.*

[Author's acknowledgment: primary references Joseph F. McCloskey's *Journal of Operations Research* papers, Vol. 35, 1, 3, 6, 1987.]

WORLD WAR II:
JAPAN'S DISINTEREST IN MERCHANT
SHIP CONVOYING

Preface

Why did Japan wait until late 1943 to implement a central broad Antisubmarine Warfare (ASW) strategy for convoying merchant shipping with escort ships and, where feasible, air cover? The Japanese Navy knew from 1939 the U-boat success with *guerre de course*, especially against merchant ships sailing independently, yet did not act.

The Setting

Japan's aggressive and successful early actions of December 1941 created within a few weeks greatly-lengthened merchant ship trade routes covering distances up to 3000 miles from the homeland.

Within eight days of Pearl Harbor, the west coast of Malaysia thousands of miles from Japan was a destination for cargo ships supporting the Japanese invasion army. The next month Singapore fell, followed later by the Philippines. Other remote invasion points all required at-sea transport over long distances. In addition to significant activity south of the home islands, the long ongoing intrusion and exploitation in northern China and Manchuria also required continuous sea transport although the distances were shorter.

On December 7, 1941, the Japanese merchant fleet stood at more than six million tons. At war, the burden of this fleet would include both the Japanese Army and Navy. Further, the fleet addressed Japan's extensive import requirements for her population as well as the huge demand for raw materials to meet extensive armament production and other industrial needs. A 20th Century island, Japan survived on imports.

Size of the Japanese Merchant Fleet

12/7/41	**6,384,000 tons**
8/14/45	**1,465,900 tons**

Accounting for the huge loss in Japanese shipping, foremost was the increasing effectiveness and skill of the United States submarine fleet, growing and improving during each year of the war. The number of United States submarines in the Pacific Theater went from 47 in 1941 to 104 in February 1943 and 169 at the end of the war in 1945. United States ships, planes and submarines had the advantage of newly-developed sonar and radar systems. Japan's military technology development and fleet implementation lagged that of the United States by four years.

Further consideration of the demise of the Japanese merchant fleet brings out other factors. The Japanese cult of the naval offensive made merchant ship convoying appear as a defensive role not in keeping with a Samurai's view of fighting on the sea. Among some naval officers, ASW study and research fell into the category of only "common sense."

It is not clear why the 20th Century Japanese Navy with its strong ties to British naval tradition, practices and strategy was not observant of Britain's success with merchant ship convoying during the last years of WWI. There is no strong evidence that convoying was an important consideration in Japan's inter-war years of naval planning.

Examination of the ASW state of readiness of Japan in late 1941 indicates ignorance of or disinterest in the heavy loss of merchant ships by Britain and others due to the improved U-boats during the first several years of WW II. Moreover, appreciation that air and sea convoy escorting of merchant ships at least moderated the losses seems to have gone unnoticed. Japan did not mount a significant focused merchant ship convoy effort until October 1943.

Before December 1941

The origins of modern Japanese naval heritage are from the successful Sino-Japanese War of 1894-5 and the Russo-Japanese War 1904-05. In both wars, success at sea came from the two Mahanian-like clashes of fleet-versus-fleet with the Battle of the Yalu in the former and the Battle of Tsushima in the latter. At that time, the industrial needs of Japan were primarily agricultural and did not demand extensive seaborne support. Japan was not unique in its naval tradition of at-sea encounters with enemy battle fleets and the consequent large budgets for battleships and supporting craft.

After the Russo-Japanese War, the Army and the Navy began to diverge gradually in their perception of national objectives. The Army opted for a continental direction to the west of Japan on mainland Asia for expansion while the Navy inclined southward in the direction of oil and rubber resources. In the years ahead, this division took a toll in national preparedness, reduced interservice cooperation, effective expenditure of resources, and, ultimately, in a rivalry for fiscal support.

Japan sided with England in WW I in accordance with an existing treaty and declared war against Germany 23 August 1914. Japan's role involved occupation of the Marshall and Caroline archipelagos and capture of Germany's Chinese port of Tsingtao in November 1914. By 1918, Japan's destroyers were part of the extensive Allied armada of support vessels in European waters in the successful convoy opposition to the U-boats.

As the fires of World War I abated in the late fall of 1918 with the armistice, attention turned to peace-making and-keeping. The new and hard-won skills of ASW and the successful protection of merchant shipping by convoying with sea and air escorts were put aside and to some extent forgotten by the primary maritime nations. Awareness of the infrequent use of highly-touted battleships by both sides during the almost five years of WW I dominated by the U-boat was forgotten. The concept of control of the sea with final decision based on the clash of great battle fleets again assumed its pre-World War I prominence among the primary powers of England, United States, France, Italy, and Japan. The battleship with its attendant high cost, long-term building requirements, manpower demands and support requirements was the weapon of choice.

In the 1920s and during the international depression period of the 1930s, economics began to play a more significant role in the restrained defense budgets of the primary maritime powers. In Japan, the actual ruling government power divided among the Army, Navy, and the Premier's cabinet with the Army in the dominant position. Further, the potential enemies were Russia, China, and United States. The Army with a strong position and military needs directed toward China and Russia in Asia met its funding needs at the expense of Navy support. With limited fiscal means and the United States as its anticipated enemy, naval strategy focused on battle groups and the decisive at-sea battles. This strategy obscured development of adequate wartime sea and air escort capabilities for shipping protection during armed conflict.

Smaller allocations insured continuing competition between Navy and Army priorities, and additional increasing attention to air power provided another factor in dividing the limited defense budgets.

Early in the 1930s, Japanese naval planning included ample recommendations for ships, boats, subchasers, air cover and wartime backup. Considerations were directed towards the need for better ASW and conversion of merchant escorts in time of war. There were other Navy voices that held opposing opinions which, when considering the U.S. as an enemy, held to the belief that enemy submarines like their own would not adopt the tactic of *guerre de course.* Budgetary restraints and lack of support prevented implementation of ASW-related developments.

In September 1940, Japan, impressed by the Axis victories in Western Europe, including the fall of France, joined the Axis powers. Germany's early 1941 success in the invasion of Soviet Russia triggered Japan's excursions in southern Asia. On July 26, Japan occupied all of French Indochina with ensuing events leading to December 7's strike at Pearl Harbor.

Major Y. Horie, former member of the Imperial Japanese Army, provides some perspective regarding a Japanese view of convoying merchant ships. Horie spent most of the war years (World War II) with the Japanese Navy, primarily concerned with the transportation of troops and materiel in his assignment with the Convoy Escort Fleet from its beginnings to its final days. Horie noted, "I found that Japanese high authority had done virtually nothing on convoy escort operation since the end of World War I." [1]

December 1941 - November 1943

The rule developed by the Allies in the battle with the U-boats based on analysis of the statistics of convoyed merchant ship losses revealed the following:

Number of escorts = (Number of merchant ships/10) + 3, if with air escort

Number of escorts x 2, if no air escort.

The importance of escorts is seen in the numbers of escorts required per convoy. Before 1940, transatlantic convoys had 2 escorts; and in 1943, the number was 7. In peacetime, no Japanese ASW escort craft were built. "The war began without a single ship designed for commerce protection on the high seas." [2]

As the war opened, the Naval General Staff placed the responsibility for shipping protection in its Operations Division with a one-officer billet. Regulations for masters of merchant ships in time of war varied, depending on the geographical locations of the ships. The Navy commanders in the various locations issued separate regulations, which created confusion. In the fall of 1942, standardized regulations appeared.

In the early part of the war, Japanese convoys of 10 to 20 merchant ships included merely one warship as escort. Further, the merchant ships went to sea unarmed. It was not until April 10, 1942, that the Japanese Navy assigned units to

---

[1] Major Y. Horie, "The Failure of the Japanese Convoy Escort," *Naval Institute Proceedings*, October 1956, p. 1073.
[2] Mark P. Parillo, *The Japanese Merchant Marine in WWII*, U. S. Naval Institute, 1993, p. 95, 97.

duty escorting merchant vessels. A shortage of adequate officer personnel to assist in this effort created difficulties. Total Japanese escort support for the 2500-mile link from Japan to Singapore consisted of 10 overage destroyers, 2 torpedo boats, and 5 merchant ships converted to gunboats. The escort for the 2000-mile passage from Yokusuka to Truk was composed of four old destroyers, one torpedo boat, and two converted gunboats.

This disarray and escort shortage created additional problems. Inadequate escort capability and independent tanker and freighter sailings did not assure the arrival in Japan of the now available and much-needed resources, particularly oil from the recently conquered areas in Southeast Asia.

In 1940, the Japanese Navy approved construction of four frigates for coastal defense. Later this class of ship provided the basic design for the much-needed and belated merchant ship convoy escorts. Initially these frigates were equipped with 12 depth charges. The reluctance to embark on an extensive escort building program did not start until mid-November 1943, when the disastrous loss of merchant ships signaled the need to provide escorts was finally realized by Japan.

Negligent in building frigates until June 1942, the Navy approved 40 frigates with a request for 360.[3]

Perspective regarding the risks of Japanese merchant shipping in July-August 1942 comes from an anecdote concerning the third war patrol of the *USS Narwhal* (SS167). This older submarine commissioned in 1930 survived the bombing at Pearl Harbor and was then the first submarine to patrol the area between Honshu and Hokkaido. On patrol the

---

[3] Atsushi Oi, "Why Japan's Antisubmarine Warfare Failed," *Naval Institute Proceedings*, June 1952, p. 592.

commanding officer Lt. Comdr. W. C. Wilkins observed the Japanese merchant ships and commented that the coastal traffic looked like "a street car line: fat targets chugging up and down the coast <u>with no escorts</u>. We could take our pick." However, Japanese ASW was not to be overlooked. Three United States submarines were lost in 1941 and 15 the following year.

By late August 1943, the Japanese Navy became alarmed because of greatly- increased merchant ship losses. The numbers of submarine attacks increased. Greater numbers of U.S. submarines equipped with communications, sonar, air and surface radar, and improved torpedoes resulted in further sinkings. Growing danger to merchant ships from American bombing planes caused additional dismay to the Japanese Navy.

Postwar accounts by Army Major Y. Horie and Navy Captain Atsushi Oi in the *U.S. Naval Institute Proceedings* addressed the basis of the inability of the Japanese Navy to cope. Oi suggests failure in ASW largely because the Navy disregarded the importance of the problem. Horie found the Navy indifferent to the problem of escort protection for merchant ships.

It became essential to confront these extreme shipping losses. On November 15, 1943, the Japanese Navy established the Grand Escort Command Headquarters with centralized responsibility over all matters of shipping protection. Frequently throughout the war years, the Navy took various steps to improve the protection of merchant ships, but always without a cohesive centralized plan, adequate manpower, and material support.

En route from Fremantle, Australia (one of seven trips), to deliver cargo and commandos to the Philippines in November, 1943, the above-mentioned *USS Narwhal* encountered what appeared to be a lone Japanese oil tanker.

However, three destroyers escorted the tanker. Packed with tons of supplies and armed only with the torpedoes in its tubes, the submarine attacked the tanker but missed. Evading the destroyer escorts, *Narwhal* went on to fulfill its mission, delivering the supplies and personnel and rescuing thirty-two.[4]

Frigates previously mentioned and called "Kaibo-kan" (coast defense), initially not intended for escort duty began to be used as merchant ship escorts. The characteristics of these 220-foot frigates of 800-1000 tons included diesel or steam engines with deck guns and 60 depth charges. Later versions carried 120 depth charges. Ranges of the order of 6000 miles were typical. Speed of 16-20 knots and adequate sonar made them almost exclusively an oceangoing convoy escort. Construction of these frigates was initiated in October 1943. By May 1944, 145 were completed. Now two years into the war, Kaibo-kans began to operate effectively in the southwest Pacific. In contrast, Britain built and had **100** convoy escorts available before the start of WWII.

Regular convoying started in mid-November 1943 but only on the Singapore run. By this time, damage to the merchant fleet was beyond repair and new construction limited. Wooden 250-ton cargo carrying sampans became numerous along the coasts as the number of merchant ships sharply decreased. Somewhat-improved convoy methods were still forthcoming the following year, 1944. Late in that year after the battle of Leyte Gulf, the Japanese Navy became a minor factor. However, it was during that fall when the U.S. lost eight submarines in six weeks, the highest rate of the war, possibly due in part to the almost after-the-fact convoy escorting of merchant ships.

---

[4] Clay Blair, Jr., *Silent Victory: The U.S. Submarine War Against Japan*, J. B. Lippincott Co., 1975, p. 497.

According to Pacific submarine war naval historian Theodore Roscoe, "Throughout the Pacific War the behavior of the Japanese escort was completely unpredictable."[5] The escort's lack of adequate communications equipment, only at this late date being equipped with primitive radar detection devices, could be one of the reasons for Roscoe's comment. In addition to the deficiency of adequate strategy and tactics for convoying, escort ships, planes, and trained personnel were in short supply.

The Technology Gap

At the start of the war, no Japanese ship was equipped with radar. It was many months before a limited number were supplied. Another year would be required to install radar on the combatant ships. The United States Navy entered the war with radar available and improvements forthcoming. The delay in the introduction of advanced technology reveals some of Japan's lag. In other systems as well, the United States continued to excel and increase Japan's technological lag even further

Japanese Technology Introduction	
1942	Shipboard radar detector
	Aircraft warning radar
1943	Battleship, medium bomber
	10cm radar
1944	Air convoy escort radar
	Escort ship radar detector (in Dec.)

---

[5] Theodore Roscoe, *United States Submarine Operations in World War*, U.S. Naval Institute, 1949, p. 216.

SUMMARY

Data from Parillo[6] display the final tonnage of the sinkings of Japanese merchant ships during the nearly four years of engagement primarily with U.S. naval forces over a wide area of the Pacific. During the years 1942-44, U.S. submarines accounted for more than 2/3 of the sinkings of Japanese merchant shipping for each of the years. At the end of 1944, remaining Japanese merchant tonnage was close to or below the 2,000,000 tons required to meet the food supply needs of the country.

Failure to consider and plan for protection of merchant shipping, particularly in view of the industrial power of the United States and the neglect of historical evidence in support of convoying, contributed greatly to the collapse of Japan. This negligence and the presence of more than 150 U.S. submarines in the Pacific by 1945 hastened Japan's defeat.

---

[6] Parillo, *op, cit*. p. 242.

Part II

Naval History

Sonobuoy

On 7 March 1942, the Navy blimp K-5, cruising over waters south of New London, Connecticut, used a new device to detect the submarine S-20, then running completely submerged. Something called a sonobuoy--a floating sonar that transmitted acoustic signals to a receiver on board the aircraft--made it possible. Improved sonobuoys were used extensively from then through the end of World War II, and 50 years later greatly enhanced sonobuoys remain one of the prime submarine detectors available to sub-hunting aircraft.

During July 1941, under the aegis of three universities--Columbia, Harvard, and California--three new naval antisubmarine laboratory research activities were established to help find ways to combat the German U-boats that had enjoyed such free rein during the early part of the war. The shipping losses for 1940 averaged about 80 per month, and this had increased to 143 per month by the end of 1942.

The successful test came only eight months after the establishment of Columbia University's antisubmarine research laboratory at Fort Trumbull, New London, Connecticut.

Russell I. Mason, a civilian engineer and a 1941 charter member of Columbia's New London Laboratory, was on board the blimp during the initial test. He stayed involved with sonobuoy developments for the next 35 years. In 1984, he observed that any list of technological developments that changed the face of naval warfare usually included radar, aircraft, submarines, radio and computers--but that sonobuoys were often omitted. Today, however, the role of the sonobuoy in antisubmarine warfare is acknowledged universally.

Columbia's efforts were concentrated at New London; Harvard's research facility was at Cambridge, Massachusetts, and the University of California began work at the Navy Radio and Sound Laboratory at Point Loma, San Diego, California. Scientists from the laboratories ranged far afield throughout the war.

The three laboratories owed their existence to a decision by Secretary of the Navy Frank Knox, who on 27 June 1940 asked the National Academy of Sciences to appoint a committee to advise him on the scientific aspects of defense against submarines and the adequacy of the Navy's preparations.

In January 1941, the committee's recommendations included the need for immediate broad scientific and engineering investigations for the development of equipment and methods involved in submarine and subsurface warfare. The committee further emphasized the importance of the selection and training of the personnel who would operate the underwater sound equipment.

Late in March 1941, the recommendations reached the General Board of the Navy. On 10 April 1941, Admiral S. M. Robinson, Chief of the Bureau of Ships, sent a letter to Dr. Vannevar Bush, Chairman of the National Defense Research Committee (NDRC), asking him to undertake an investigation of submarine detection. The commands to be supported by the laboratories included submarine and destroyer forces in the Atlantic and Pacific, Army Air Force, Royal Canadian Air Force, and the Fleet Air Arm of the Royal Navy.

James Phinney Baxter III, the historian of the Navy's Office of Research and Development, in his 1946 Pulitzer Prize-winning official historian Scientists Against Time, said of the sonobuoy: "Developed with infinite skill and thoroughness, and sent into operation thorough most intimate cooperation between the New London Laboratory and Air Force, Atlantic Fleet, the expendable sono-radio buoy became one of the outstanding developments of the war."

The earliest proposal for an expendable sonic buoy was made by Dr. P. M. S. Blackett, a senior British physicist broadly involved in the war effort, who in May 1941 wrote a memorandum proposing a detector buoy astern of convoys to detect shadowing or trailing enemy submarines. Some of Bush's scientists apparently learned about the proposal while in Great Britain on an exchange mission concerning antisubmarine devices.

The British government, under the auspices of NDRC, subsequently requested the Radio Corporation of America (RCA) to develop a medium-life, ship-launched convoy-type radio sonobuoy. The New London Laboratory was responsible for the testing, and by 12 September 1941, RCA had units ready for testing at sea. The electrical performance of the buoy was excellent, but the Navy rejected it because of its limited acoustic range. The remaining experimental models were used to great advantage, however, during the development of the aircraft-type buoy.

In December 1941, the laboratory was asked to develop a hydrophone for use with the harbor protection radio sonobuoy authorized by the Navy. Efforts were successful, and a large quantity of these devices were manufactured under Navy contract and later used extensively at advanced bases.

In February 1942, the Navy's interest in sonobuoy was rekindled by a need to improve the ASW capabilities of coastal-patrol blimps, which were using early versions of magnetic anomaly detector (MAD) equipment to distinguish live submarines from submerged wrecks along the coast. The New London Laboratory investigated both a dropped radio sonobuoy and a hydrophone towed from a blimp.

All of this led to the breakthrough on 7 March. The blimp did not actually make the drop. Two modified RCA buoys, left over from the previous tests, were placed in the waster by a launch. The sonobuoy was able to detect the submarine S-20's underwater sounds at ranges up to three miles. In turn, the receiver on the K-5 picked up the sonobuoy transmissions easily while cruising within five miles. This particular test moved the sonobuoy into the first rank of detectors.

Mason operated the receiver on board the blimp K-5; he, J. C. McNary, and V. V. Graf submitted the test report. During his career, Mason received 16 patents, including one for the original airborne sonobuoy.

Not long after, the U.S. Army Air Corps, heavily engaged in antisubmarine flights off the East Coast, became interested in the sonobuoy. As a result of the interest and encouragement by a Colonel Dolan of the Sea Search Group operating out of Langley, Virginia, sonobuoys were altered at New London for aircraft instead of blimp delivery. By 25 July 1942, an aircraft had successfully launched a sonobuoy.

Mason, reflecting on this episode in 1984, said, "[By]…August 1942, Colonel Dolan expended sonobuoys in actual off-shore operations against U-boats. The success...caused the Army to order 6,410 buoys in late 1942."

Additional Navy blimp tests had proved successful, sonobuoys were ordered in quantity in mid-1942; and operations employing sonobuoys began in August. More than 400 experimental buoys and 30 receivers were contracted to the Emerson Radio and Phonograph Corporation, General Electric Company, and the Freed Radio Corporation.

By June 1943, the expendable radio sonobuoy had been officially approved by the Navy for use on all planes and blimps engaged in antisubmarine warfare. Later in 1944 and 1945, sonobuoy use extended to include air-sea rescue operations for airmen downed in the Pacific.

Columbia University's final report includes an individual description of all the New London Laboratory's projects, a summary of patent reports, and an index of documents for the period 15 September 1941 to 30 June 1945. The laboratory undertook more than 80 projects during this period.

Samuel Eliot Morison identified the importance of the sonobuoy to the Normandy invasion in The Two-Ocean War: "[An] entire portion of the channel was inspected by a plane every 35 minutes. All had microwave radar and sonobuoys to drop...not one of the 58 U-boats Donitz alerted...got near the invasion area."

The 26 months from March 1942 to the Normandy invasion in June 1944 was a comparatively short time to develop, manufacture and field what turned out to be one of the decisive tools in the confrontation with the U-boats. They had come a long way since Mason tested the first units by dropping them from a Thames River bridge in New

London and a Connecticut River bridge in Middletown—on one occasion leading a Federal Communications Commission radio monitoring site to suspect clandestine spy transmissions.

The 29 October 1948 issue of the New London Underwater Sound Laboratory bi-weekly Bulletin contained the first account of the adventures of the three New London Laboratory civilian engineers whose field work with the sonobuoy led them into combat areas. Mason's tenure with sonobuoy during the war extended from February 1942 until June 1945. His overseas assignments carried him to every continent except Asia. The other two members of the triumvirate, Russell Lewis and Walter Clearwaters, came from Purdue University and were on board and involved with sonobuoys by 1943.

Lewis was assigned to the group that introduced the sonobuoy to the Navy. In early summer 1943—accompanied by Mason—his first field trip took him to Argentia, Newfoundland, where VB-103 was preparing for antisubmarine escort duty in the mid-North Atlantic that would close a gap hitherto unprotected from the air. The squadron's aircraft were equipped with radar, long-range navigation (Loran), guns, depth charges and sonobuoys. During their time with the squadron both men participated in many 14-16 hour patrols to the middle of the North Atlantic and back, flying antisubmarine sweeps ahead of the convoys.

By September, Lewis had helped Fleet Air Wing 7 prepare for sweeps over the Bay of Biscay and the English Channel. Following this, he went on to Hawaii, and by November was in Bermuda. January 1944 found him flying ASW patrols from the escort carrier USS Block Island (CVE-21) off Portugal and the Azores. On 29 May 1944, the carrier was torpedoed by the German submarine U-549—later sunk herself by the carrier's escorts—and Lewis spent several hours in the water along with the other survivors before being picked up by a destroyer and taken to Casablanca. His globe trotting continued until March 1945. He spent more than 2,500 hours in the air on tests, travel and operations. He made 19 transoceanic flights, survived four crashes and was awarded a Navy commendation.

In June 1943, Clearwaters and Price Fish, also from the New London Laboratory, went to Iceland to install sonobuoy equipment in the planes of patrol Squadron 63 in preparation for combat operations in European waters. They accompanied the squadron to South Pembroke, Wales, and flew on submarine-hunting missions.

Back in Iceland in late September, Clearwaters participated in an antisubmarine flight with the Royal Canadian Air Force on which the crew successfully engaged a German submarine, providing an opportunity for Clearwaters to use sonobuoys in the air attack. His next stop was the escort carrier USS Bogue (CVE-9), and then it was on to Casablanca. In early 1945, he completed his sonobuoy work as a member of the laboratory team that participated in extensive tests off Fort Lauderdale, Florida.

By war's end in summer 1945, the Navy had ordered 150,000 expendable sonobuoys and 7,500 receivers. The Royal Canadian Air Force, the Royal Air Force, and the Fleet Air Arm of the Royal Navy also employed the equipment.

The work on the sonobuoy concluded with the administrative changes in the Laboratory that took place in 1945. There was some continuing industrial interest, and the Naval Air Development Center at Warminster, Pennsylvania, evolved as a focus for the sonobuoy during the 1950s. The United States, Canada, and Great Britain continued to pursue their interests in airborne antisubmarine warfare. Sonobuoys were standardized among the three countries, later joined by Australia and New Zealand.

Today, the literature on antisubmarine warfare reflects the continuing recognition of the importance of the sonobuoy. In 1989, Captain W. T. T. Pakenham described sonobuoys as "…a most valuable method of harnessing the mobility of aircraft for antisubmarine warfare." He also included reference to the important use of sonobuoys in conjunction with helicopters. Much of the success of the ASW helicopter can be traced to the effectiveness of current-day sonobuoys.

Fifty-two years later, the lineal descendants of the World War II development are still on the front line.

From the Heavens to the Depths

Early in World War I, the science community in he United States began to recognize shortcomings in the country's ability to defend against German U-boat operations. Distinguished solar astronomer George Ellery Hale ---here at left, with Robert A. Millikan, chairman of the National Research Council's Physics Committee---orchestrated a partnership between science and industry in the U. S. Military that accelerated the Allied antisubmarine warfare effort.*

In 1915, the second year of World War I, U.S. military preparedness shortcomings caught the attention of George Ellery Hale, known worldwide for his research in solar astronomy. Sensing an opportunity for support of scientific research, he ultimately succeeded in bringing together, for the first time, engineers and scientists from U.S. industry and academia to

*California Institute of Technology Archives

address a broad array of challenges related to upgrading military preparedness prior to and following the entry of the United States into the war in April 1917.

Among several critical areas of concern was the need to develop new methods to counter the increasingly successful German U-boat offensive. The paramount problem of detecting enemy submarines presented itself shortly after the start of the war and continues to this day. Although Hale's work in astronomy and his influence upon the evolving field of astrophysics far overshadowed his efforts toward improving U.S. military preparedness from 1915-1918, these contributions were significant, nonetheless.

In 1914, the world's 16 leading navies had more than 400 submarines. Initially, these were underrated, considered useful only for defensive roles. But early German success in submarine commerce raiding and naval sinkings confirmed that they were quickly becoming an important new offensive class of fighting ship.

At the start of the war, Germany had 25 U-boats (10 at sea) and more under construction. Alarm over their effectiveness heightened with the realization that, even though they were vulnerable to mines, virtually no method was in place for their detection when submerged.

In 1915, Congress sought technological initiatives for military preparedness, and Hale saw a role in this respect for the National Academy of Sciences (NAS) membership as well as other scientists. He suggested that the academy offer its services to President Woodrow Wilson in the event of war with Mexico or Germany.

The U-20 sinking of the Lusitania on 7 May 1915, with loss of 1,200 lives (including 128 U.S. citizens), shocked the nation and the world. Two months later, Hale wrote to NAS President William H. Welch of Johns Hopkins University regarding the government's need for scientific services and his vision of offering the academy's membership to help. Members advised that such action might be premature; maintaining a neutral role was a continuing problem for the administration. But President Wilson recognized the importance of science in war and need to apply science both to industrial and military problems. Hale felt that, "…this is the greatest chance we have ever had to advance research in America. The spirit of national service in the air coupled with the desire for preparedness should make everything possible."[1]

Congress responded to the Lusitania sinking by establishing two technological groups, the Naval Consulting Board (NCB) and the National Advisory Committee on Aeronautics in July 1915. Membership of the NCB consisted primarily of senior inventors and engineers but included neither the membership of the NAS nor the American Physical Society (primarily physicists).

Legislative action the following March (the Defense Act of 1916) provided additional presidential powers concerning preparedness and national defense and established the Council of National Defense, with full cabinet membership and responsibility for national security and welfare.

From the start of the war, Hale believed that the United States eventually would abandon neutrality. While his two apparent intentions were to have NAS scientists contribute to military preparedness and to initiate a government and science relationship that eventually would continue in peacetime, government patronage was not one of Hale's goals.

---

[1] Robert H. Kargon, *The Rise of Robert Millikan: Portrait of a Life in American Science* (Ithaca, NY: Cornell University Press 1982), p. 83.

The torpedoing of the French cross-channel packet Sussex by a U-boat on 24 March 1916, which left 80 dead and two Americans wounded, brought about the President's ultimatum to Germany on 18 April against unrestricted German submarine warfare. The incident caused a further general burst of outrage from Congress and others. The day after the ultimatum, Hale presented a resolution to the NAS annual meeting in Washington, D.C., offering the services of the academy to the President. Hale's idea was to establish a National Research Council (NRC) of representatives from ongoing scientific organizations in the United States: the American Academy for the Advancement of Science, the Smithsonian Institution, and the NAS. The academy accepted the resolution, and Hale chaired an organizing committee. A committee also was appointed to call on President Wilson.

Regarding Hale's approach to government involvement, Daniel J. Kelves observed in The Physicists that "he intended that the Council, a private body like its parent, the National Academy, perform a public function, the mobilization of science for defense, without governmental oversight."[2]

The new war focused attention quickly on its scientific and technological aspects. Unlike previous wars, the almost worldwide scale of this one and its effective sea blockades created problems requiring quick solutions. The government did not support scientists in a way that would ensure attention to significant military and industry problems. Working primarily as individuals those in the science community were not focused solely on military preparedness needs. With this background, Hale began the task of introducing scientists to military needs and persuading the military to work with scientists.

---

[2] Daniel J. Kelves, *The Physicists* (New York : Alfred A. Knopf, 1978), p 117.

When Hale and other NAS members met with President Wilson 26 April, Wilson immediately expressed interest in the concept of their aid, but he was cautious regarding how to proceed. The group decided that the NAS would form a committee, with a public announcement to come later.

On 4 May 1916 Germany's response to President Wilson's ultimatum reached Washington. It was the so-called Sussex Pledge, agreeing to restrict submarine warfare to belligerents. But the number of U-boats continued to increase. By the end of 1916 the Germans had built 102, with 38 on station, with 8 merchant submarines.

The following month, the National Academy formalized the NRC, and Hale obtained a promise of cooperation from leading scientific societies, schools of technology, heads of universities, medicine, research foundations, and industrial laboratories. The White House approved of the NRC publicly on 24 July. The next day, President Wilson wrote to NAS President Welch (with a copy to Hale), indicating his approval of the NRC's plans and his active assistance in completing its organization.

A 29 July letter from Hale to The New York Times stated that NRC working committees were either completely or partially organized and were at work on scientific and technical areas relating to the nation's nitric acid supply, preventative medicine, organic chemicals, and military communications. Other military-related assignments evolved later.

Before the United States entered the war on 6 April 1917, NRC fiscal support came from the universities and private sources. The Engineering Foundation applied its entire income for the year to the NRC and provided a New York office. The Carnegie and Rockefeller foundations also were important benefactors. NRC organizational meetings were held, and on 21 September, The New York Times reported that the purpose of the NRC was the development of applied science to strengthen national defense, involving existing government, educational, industrial, and other research organizations. The NRC included on its roster the chiefs of the technical bureaus of the Army and the Navy. A Hale biographer notes: "Now, under Hale's leadership, American scientists would have the chance to develop cooperative research on an unparalleled scale, first for war and later, as he had hoped and planned from the beginning, for peace. From this time science was to become an increasingly powerful force in American Life."3

Germany honored the Sussex Pledge until 1 February 1917, when it renewed its unrestricted submarine warfare. The break between the United States and Germany took place on 3 February, and arming of U.S. merchant ships commenced on the 26th. At that time, the United States began to share the submarine problem that had been plaguing the Allies for more than 18 months. Learning to detect, locate, and destroy U-boats was primary and time-critical. The supporting shipbuilding program indicated the scale of the overall effort to counter the U-boats. New destroyers and submarine chasers alone accounted for an expenditure of more than $500 million.4 The President's Council of National Defense requested Hale's NRC to act as its scientific department. A few days after Germany's scrapping of the Sussex Pledge, submarine-related problems became the NRC's primary Navy focus.

Antisubmarine research efforts were under way prior to the declaration of war under the advocacy of the Council. At Columbia University, Dr. M. I. Pupin and other NRC scientists began an investigation into the use of supersonic frequencies in submarine location. Dr. R. A. Millikan, chairman of the Physics Committee, conducted research at the Western Electric Laboratories in Manhattan.

At the end of March, the NRC sent a mission to Europe to gain insight into the wartime technical efforts of England, France, and Italy. Chaired by Joseph S. Ames of Johns Hopkins, ten scientists departed for Europe early in April. The Ames mission provided an account of the dire nature of the Allies' military situation and their heavy dependence on U.S. efforts for survival. The trip apparently also encouraged the May 1917 visit of English and French scientists to the United States for an exchange of information regarding the development of antisubmarine devices. The group included Ernest Rutherford, 1904 Nobel laureate. Hale hosted the exchange team.

David Wilson, a Rutherford biographer, concluded that probably the biggest single result of Rutherford's mission was the recommendation for setting up a new second experimental antisubmarine research at New London, Connecticut.5

Sound, light, heat, and electricity were considered as detection techniques. By the time the war ended, ten main U.S. antisubmarine research centers had been established, eight of which were supported by the NRC, and were located at universities, industrial laboratories, and at the Navy Yard in Key West, Florida.

In mid-1917, the NRC scientists took over an abandoned building adjacent to the Fort Trumbull U. S. Coast Guard military reservation on the west bank of the Thames River in New London. Experiments included Navy planes and dirigibles; Navy seaplanes were located on an adjacent cove. A marine railway also was rebuilt. Among the research facilities were three submarine chasers, a destroyer and three converted steam yachts; submarines were assigned to the station as required.

Scientific staff of Experimental Station New London, Connecticut, assembled for a photo ten days after the Armistice that ended World War 1. Third from left in the front row is Max Mason, the University of Wisconsin mathemetician who invented an underwater sound detector "considered in some circles to be the best of those available to the Allied nations."

Above picture of Scientific Staff, November 21, 1918

Back row: Frank Gray, G.G. Bidwell, O.O. Kellogg, J..R. Roebuck, P. W. Bridgman (Nobel Laureate), Geo. E. Stebbins, H. M. Trueblood, R. R. Ireland, W. T. Coyle Front Row: H. C. Hayes, G. W. Pierce, Max Mason, Captain J. R. Defrees USN, Ernest Merritt, E.M. Hewlett, H. B. Smith

A total of 12 NRC academic scientists, including two future Nobel physics laureates, conducted research. Among the universities represented were Chicago, Cornell, Columbia, Harvard, McGill, Massachusetts Institute of Technology, Rice, Swarthmore, Tufts, Wesleyan, Wisconsin and Yale. Vannevar Bush, later Chairman of the National Research Council during World War II, also conducted antisubmarine research in New London. By January 1918, more than 200 people were at the New London Station, and by the time of the signing of the Armistice in November, that number had grown to more than 700.

Navy fiscal support became available in October 1917, as Assistant Secretary of the Navy Franklin D. Roosevelt expedited the transfer of $300,000 to what had been designated as the Navy Experimental Station at New London. By war's end, nearly $1 million funded the Station.

In early July 1917, Max Mason, a member of the research team and a noted mathematician from the University of Wisconsin, invented and conducted experiments with an underwater sound detector. At the end of the hostilities, Mason's detector was considered in some circles to be the best of those available to the Allied nations.

The Experimental Station at New London closed at the end of World War I. As the German submarine threat again became menacing in World War II, however, many of the World War I NRC scientists provided the core of Vannevar Bush's 1940 committee and were instrumental in seeing the Fort Trumbull area again become a high technology site for antisubmarine efforts. This laboratory continued as the Navy's premiere antisubmarine laboratory until 1997.

As early as February 1918, Hale, Millikan and various members of the scientific community engaged in the war effort began to consider continuing the NRC and its governmental relationships on a permanent basis. At Hale's initiative, on 11 May 1918 President Wilson signed an executive order providing for the Council's perpetuation in peacetime.

Hale succeeded in continuing the NRC into the postwar era and beyond. The NRC had reached the status Hale had wanted, that of keeping pure and applied science together in one organization and outside the Federal government. The Council's effectiveness, however, would be constrained by limited fiscal support and authority. Hale continued his NRC chairmanship until May 1919, when he resigned and was made permanent honorary chairman.

With the war's formal end six months later, the NRC looked back at either success or progress in a wide variety of technological areas, including gun battery sound ranging, physiology of battlefield shock, preventive medicine, organic chemicals, submarine-detection devices, bomb-dropping techniques, aerial photography, aeronautic instrumentation, radio telephone, wireless communication between airplanes, infrared and ultraviolet signaling, antipersonnel gases, gas masks, optical glass and ballistic tables for Army projectiles.

The NRC achieved cooperation between rival Federal agencies and obtained the respect of the bureau chiefs of the Army and the Navy. These efforts brought increased national awareness of the importance of science, the expanded role of scientists in society, and science as a career.

Hale brought the NRC into being motivated by his perception of the need for scientists to contribute to the escalating preparedness needs in the years immediately before World War I. In retrospect, the Council was limited by funding and authority. Its shortcomings and their impact on the war effort did not go unnoticed by the participating scientists. Senior scientists facing the problems of World War II 20 years later were able to organize better nationally with the military and industry. During the subsequent five-year war, this proved essential.

Undoubtedly, Hale is remembered best for his contributions to astronomy. In 1902, at age 33, he was elected to the NAS. His observations of sunspot spectra in 1908 and subsequent analysis showed for the first time the presence of magnetic fields in sunspots and an extra-terrestrial magnetic field. His legacy in the form of the National Research Council, however, had broad and lasting ramifications for the country and for all of its scientists.

Part III

IEEE Oceanic Engineering News Letter

Harvard Underwater Sound Laboratory

The Harvard Underwater Sound Laboratory (HUSL) operated under the auspices of the National Defense Research Committee (NDRC) from 5 June 1941 to 31 January 1946. Frederick V. Hunt, a professor of physics and communications engineering at Harvard, served as the laboratory's director during the entire period. Hunt started with a small staff: by the end of July 1942, the total number of employees was about 125. A peak of about 462 was reached in August 1944. More than half of research associates held advanced degrees in physics and electrical engineering. There were 39 research associates from Massachusetts with 116 coming from all other states. The facilities grew to accommodate the needs. In addition to locations away from Massachusetts such as the testing field station in Fort Lauderdale, Florida, where opportunities for sea tests on more days per year were possible, there were others in the Boston area. A barge calibration station was established in the Charles River Basin. In nearby Arlington, Massachusetts, a calibration station was established on Spy Pond.

The Laboratory made use of a fleet of seven test craft, including yachts, motor sailers, a launch and two barges. Other ship facilities provided by the Navy included submarine chasers, destroyer escorts, destroyers, and various naval aircraft.

As cited in the Harvard Laboratory final report,[1] the first phase of the work was to pursue developments which would increase the effectiveness of existing submarine detection equipment already installed in the ships of the fleet. Further, the program was to include investigation and experimentation with new forms of submarine detection equipment which would offer the possibility of improved submarine detection and location. The program was broadened in the fall of 1941 by the start of work which might lead to the antisubmarine torpedo or mine which would steer itself automatically toward the sound produced by a target submarine.

It is interesting to note that Hunt is attributed with originating the term "sonar" in February 1942 during the time he was visiting at the University of California Sound Laboratory in San Diego, California. Eventually the term was defined as "Sound Navigation and Ranging" to make it the acoustic equivalent of radar. Shortly after the term had been coined, Hunt and Lt. Commander C. L. Engleman of the Bureau of Ships proposed that term designate ratings trained as sound operators as "sonar men." The word "sonar" was approved for general use and given its modern meaning in the U.S. Fleet A/S Bulletin for November 1943. The term refers to both passive sonar (meaning listening) and to active sonar (meaning echo-ranging techniques). A 1970 discussion of acoustics during the 1941-1945 period by Hunt at a national convocation of acousticians identified

---

[1] Hunt, F. V. *Final Report for Contract OEMsr-58 and Contract OEMSr-287. 1941-1946. Applied Acoustic and Subsurface Warfare*. OSRD Div. 6 prepared by the Underwater Sound Library Harvard University. Cambridge MA. January 31, 1946

many of the areas of research and development which were in the purview of the Harvard Laboratory.[2] The areas included the design of directional listening arrays, establishing and demonstrating the advantages of scanning sonar, and the development of the acoustic torpedo, the first homing missile of any type to become operational. In the aggregate, during the four and one-half years it operated, the Laboratory investigated and reported on about sixty studies and projects.

The significant increase in enemy submarine activity on the United States east coast during the first six months of 1942 provided additional impetus to the developments of improvements immediately applicable to sonar equipment already installed on convoy escort vessels. The Laboratory also assisted the manufacturers in the production of new devices needed for the improvements. In addition, Harvard provided support to the Navy in the installations of the new devices and in the training of naval personnel in the implementation of the changes made in the submarine detection equipments.

An important example of the various projects assigned to the Harvard Laboratory comes from one requested by the Bureau of Ordnance in November 1941. The Laboratory was asked to consider the problem of developing an air-launched acoustic antisubmarine mine (torpedo). As early as 1933, the Germans had shown interest in the development of the tactical innovation of an acoustic torpedo. By the spring of 1943, the Laboratory developed and tested a mine that was then operationally deployed. The concept was to have this air-launched and self-propelled weapon capable of homing on the noise produced by a submerged submarine target. In addition to the Laboratory,

[2] Hunt, F. V. "The Past Twenty Years in Underwater Acoustics: Introductory Retrospection." *Journal of the Acoustical Society of America.* Vol. 51. No. 3 (part 2). 1972.

other naval and industrial organizations were involved in the development. In particular, collaboration with the Bell Telephone Laboratories was significant.

The first U-boat sinking using the newly-developed mine (designated MK24) took place on 14 May 1943 in the Atlantic. Two U-boats were sunk, one by an MK24 from a Liberator (B-245) and one from a U.S. Navy Catalina (PBY).

Another example of extensive work undertaken by the Harvard laboratory is the development of a torpedo for use by submarines against enemy warships and merchant vessels. The task, stemming from the Bureau of Ordnance, was for development of a full-size submarine-launched electric torpedo adapted for acoustic homing on the noise generated by the target vessel. The scale of this effort is seen by noting that the submarine torpedo is a 21-foot cylinder weighing 1.5 tons. Some of the collaboration was with Bell Telephone Laboratories and the Westinghouse Corporation. Intense efforts included investigation and reduction of the self-noise of the torpedo and the development of unique hydrophones. By 10-11 October 1945, successful acoustic steering of a full-size high-speed torpedo was obtained in tests conducted off Nahant, Massachusetts. The hundreds of bibliographic reports and internal memoranda on the acoustic torpedo are dated from July 1943 to January 1946.

Scanning sonar was one of the Harvard Laboratory's major development projects. Studies and related projects for advancing this concept occurred as early as 1942 and continued until mid-1945. The object of this work was to provide a form of sonar equipment that would be continuously alert in all directions and furnish a continuous indication of the position of all underwater sound-reflecting objects within detection range. Systems suitable for both submarines and surface craft application were studied and developed.

The work progressed, but scanning sonar did not reach the production stage to permit installation of commercially-built equipment in the fleet during the war. One experimental scanning sonar installation was operational on the USS Semmes (AG24) which participated with several other antisubmarine vessels in a successful attack on a German submarine off Cape Cod, Massachusetts.

About the time of the end of World War II, the Harvard Laboratory torpedo development program was transferred to Pennsylvania State College, State College, Pennsylvania, where the Navy at that time established an Ordnance Research Laboratory (later known as the Applied Research Laboratory). The transfer of this effort from Cambridge to Pennsylvania occurred between August and October 1945. Many of the persons who had been engaged at the Harvard Laboratory in the torpedo development program moved to the new laboratory.

During this period, the Harvard Laboratory programs on training and on certain items of test equipment were transferred to the U.S. Navy Radio and Sound Laboratory at San Diego, California. With the Laboratory's surface ship sonar development program transferred to the Navy Underwater Sound Laboratory at New London, Connecticut and the torpedo development program at the Ordnance Research Laboratory at Pennsylvania State College, in January 1946 the final NDRC contract with Harvard University was completed.

University of California
Division of War Research at San Diego

Responding to the submarine problem, the Office of Scientific Research and Development (OSRD) and the National Defense Research Committee (NDRC) contracted with the University of California on 21 April 1941 to organize a laboratory responsible for "a broad research program covering the fundamentals of every aspect of the problem."[1] With many other additional assignments, the University of California division of War Research (UCDWR) continued until 30 June 1946. The laboratory location at the U. S. Navy Radio and Sound Laboratory (NRSL), Point Loma, San Diego, California, was chosen because of its proximity to deep water and because of the number days per year that would be favorable to research at seas. The oceanography of the California coast had already been studied extensively by the nearby Scripps Institute of Oceanography in La Jolla just north of San Diego. The Navy had also established a sound school in San Diego in 1939 for the training of sound detection equipment operators (later sonar operators). The school eventually was equipped to handle as many as 1,200 students. During the war years, the combined laboratories were informally known by the Navy and others as the San Diego Laboratory.

At its wartime peak, NRSL had a staff of about 150 civilians; UCDWR's staff was approximately 575. The NRSL staff was expanded by radar and radio experts from

---

[1] National Research Council, *Principles of Underwater Sound*, Washington, D.C., 1968, preface

the Naval Research Laboratory (NRL) in Anacostia, Maryland. The staff at NRSL was further supplemented by Navy officers and petty officers called back from retirement.

Like the staff at both Columbia and Harvard sound laboratories, that at UCDWR had wide scientific, technical and industrial backgrounds. In San Diego, proximity to the Scripps Institute provided an excellent source of consultants and personnel. As in the case of New London's staffing, several research personnel from the electrical recording and projecting of sound were recruited from the movie industry in Hollywood, California.

In addition to personnel from Scripps, the University of California at Los Angeles and Berkeley, California Institute of Technology, Brigham Young University, and other academic institutions were represented on the staff of the Point Loma Laboratory.

The first director of UCDWR was Dr. Vern Knudsen from the University of California at Los Angeles. Dr. H. U. Sverdrup, Director of Scripps, in 1941 organized the Oceanographic Section at Point Loma. The new laboratory was divided into three major parts: sonar training, sonar devices, and sonar data, each division addressing a particular aspect of the sound and the submarine problem.

In late 1941, under OSRD the Navy started construction of various structures designed to be temporary. Construction continued during the next several years in which facilities for laboratories, machine ships, library, drafting, and publications were brought to fruition.

Specialized facilities, for UCDWR-designed transducers and acoustic homing torpedoes, used a barge anchored in San Diego Bay. Later in 1943, the Navy began using Sweetwater Lake, 17 miles southeast of Point Loma.

At the San Diego Laboratory, important areas of effort included sonar research, basic research in oceanography, and field engineering support to U.S. submarines.

The Sonar Data Division accumulated scientific data on underwater sound for nearly five years. The information collected provided data on background noise in the sea, the propagation of underwater sound, and its attenuation. This led to effective use of existing underwater sound equipment and an ability to predict how the equipment would perform in varying situations. In addition, the new knowledge about underwater sound was made available to both sonar schools and the Fleet, to teach personnel how to use sonar more effectively to detect and attack submarines. Further, the same knowledge was also used to teach U. S. submarines how to evade enemy sonar.

The development of scanning sonar (continuous display of all underwater objects within acoustical detection range) was pursued at San Diego as well as at the Harvard Underwater Sound Laboratory. A scanning sonar developed at the laboratory was tested early in 1944 in the Mediterranean and was successful in detecting the presence of mines. This was the first sonar to provide a plot display of multiple targets and to offer a capability as a moored-mine detector. By the summer of 1945, forty-eight sonars of this type were with the submarine fleet. In the final months of the war, U. S. submarines equipped with this sonar effectively severed communications between the five main islands of Japan.

Similarly to the case at the New London Laboratory, the efforts at San Diego included both antisubmarine and prosubmarine programs, the latter beginning in early 1943. The prosubmarine program involved over half of the Laboratory's staff. Field engineering was emphasized, with

UCDWR representatives in the Pacific area being attached to the Submarine Command almost continuously.

In 1945, NRSL at San Diego was renamed the U.S. Naval Electronics Laboratory (NEL) on 29 November. The following year, on 30 June 1946, UCDWR's remaining projects and contracts were absorbed and continued by NEL. Many UCDWR employees transferred to NEL. A certain portion of work also came to NEL from incomplete work being done at the Massachusetts Institute of Technology and, as previously mentioned, some of the residual efforts from the Harvard Laboratory.

Placed under the Bureau of Ships, NEL was tasked "to effectuate the solution of any problem in the field of electronics, in connection with the design, procurement, testing, installation and maintenance of electronic equipment for a the U.S. Navy."[2]

---

[2] Naval Ocean Systems Center, *Fifty Years of Research and Development on Point Loma 1940-1990*. San Diego, CA. 1990. p. 24.